INTERROGATING CHILD PROBLEMS

About the Authors

Pankaj Kumar is Head, Department of Sociology, Asansol Girls' College, Kazi Nazrul University (KNU), West Bengal. He has completed his M.A. from Jawaharlal Nehru University, M.Phil. from Delhi University and Ph.D. from University of Burdwan (W.B.). He has published several research papers in edited books and referred journals. He has presented several research papers in various state and national seminars and workshops. He has published a edited book on gender issue. His work has focused on the development induced displacement, tribal, women and child.

Sadhna Gupta (WBES) is Assistant Professor in Department of Law, Hooghly Mohsin Govt. College, West Bengal. She completed her Bachelor and Master of Laws and Ph.D. from the Burdwan University, West Bengal. She specialized in Human Rights and Gender Justice and did her Ph.D. on "Trafficking and Prostitution". Child and Women related issues are her special areas of interest. Her research papers are published in different research journals of national and international repute touching upon various aspects of human rights issues. She has published a edited book titled '*Relocating Women's Equality*'.

INTERROGATING CHILD PROBLEMS
Issues and Challenges

Pankaj Kumar
Sadhna Gupta

CONCEPT PUBLISHING COMPANY PVT. LTD.
NEW DELHI-110059

ISBN-13 : 978-93-5125-223-8

First Published 2016

Published and Printed by

Concept
Since 1974

Concept Publishing Company Pvt. Ltd.
A/15-16, Commercial Block, Mohan Garden
New Delhi-110059 (India)
T: 25351460, 25351794, *F*: 091-11-25357109
E: publishing@conceptpub.com, W: www.conceptpub.com
Editorial Office: H-13, Bali Nagar, New Delhi-110 015, India.

Cataloging in Publication Data--*Courtesy:* D.K. Agencies (P) Ltd. <docinfo@dkagencies.com>

Kumar, Pankaj, author.
Interrogating child problems : issues and challenges / Pankaj Kumar, Sadhna Gupta.
pages cm
Includes bibliographical references and index.
ISBN 9789351252238

1. Children's rights--India. 2. Children--Legal status, laws, etc.--India. 3. Children--Crimes against--India. 4. Girls--Crimes against--India. I. Gupta, Sadhna, author. II. Title.

KNS517.K86 2016 DDC 346.5408772 23

PREFACE

The Convention on the Rights of the Child, 1989 under Article 3 rightly stated that the nation's children are a supremely important asset. The Government of India even in the National Policy for Children No. 1-14/74-CDD had accepted too. Their nurture and solicitude are our responsibility. Children's programme should find prominent part in our National Plan for the development of human resources so that our children grow-up to become robust citizen, physically fit, mentally alert and morally healthy, endowed with the skills and motivations provided by society.

India is a home to about 430 million children and as a consequence rights of children and their aspirations are of paramount importance in our march towards an inclusive and equitable society. No nation can afford to ignore children because they are a national asset. At the same time, they are the weakest and most vulnerable segment of the society. Since Independence, India has developed its own jurisprudence concerning children and the recognition of their privileges. Our Constitution guarantees several special privileges to children, such as free and compulsory primary education to children between the age group of six to fourteen years, prohibition of trafficking and forced labour of children and prohibition of employment of children below the age of fourteen years in factories, mines or hazardous occupations. In succinct, the Constitution of India is wholly committed to combat the exploitation of children in any form. It shall be the policy of the State to provide adequate services to children, both before and after birth and through the period of growth, to ensure their full physical, mental and social development.

The issues addressed in this book include — child sexual abuse, child labour, mid-day meal scheme, stalking, child pornography and other child concerned topics. The focus of this book is on child problems and its solution through law enforcement agencies. The range of topics covered in this book should be of broad interest to professionals working in the field of child problems and child rights.

We are extremely grateful to Professor (Dr.) Biswajit Ghosh (Department of Sociology, University of Burdwan) and Professor

(Dr.) Manik Chakrabarty (Department of Law, University of Burdwan) who gave us time, guidance and support at various stages of preparation of this work.

We are grateful to our colleagues for providing peaceful environment to make this work possible. Through this book we also acknowledge the love and affection rendered to us by our students, their appreciation and admiration is an important source of encouragement and motivation.

The support given by our children, Pooja and Sristi is also remembered with thanks. We express gratitude to our parents, relatives and friends who have encouraged our academic activities. Last, but not the least, we express our thanks and appreciation to Concept Publishing Co. Pvt. Ltd., New Delhi for publishing this book under extreme care, precision and patience.

Pankaj Kumar
Sadhna Gupta

CONTENTS

LIST OF TABLES

INTRODUCTION

"The development of children is the first priority on the country's development agenda, not because they are the most vulnerable, but because they are our supreme assets and also the future human resources of the country."

Tenth Five Year Plan (2002-07)

Child by an adjective phrase means "a person who is unable to maintain itself". Childhood is a universal human experience. Because of their age and lack of experience children are the most vulnerable group of society. With such a vast size of the child population (Children in the age group of 0 to 18 years would number approximately 400 million, constituting about 40 per cent of the population) and evidently from different socio-economic background, in a developing economy like India, the vulnerability of children is bound to increase. This obviously leads to higher demand on the state to make specific efforts to create facilities which are essential for the healthy growth of the children as future citizens and human resources of the country (Gautam, 2006:25). In every child, the foundation of a nation is laid. The proper development of the child is, therefore, imperative for the proper growth of a nation. The protection and welfare is of utmost importance to the society. Children are unable to raise their voice against those who injure them. It is for this reason, that a society must have two concerns which are —

(a) Children being the most delicate yet best human resource for future, they require growth, development and best care; and
(b) Children being most vulnerable, they are to be protected from all sorts of exploitation — physical, mental and moral (Choudhary, 2004:1).

Children are the human resources and assets of a nation. A nation's health is gauged through the health of its children. It is, therefore, essential that children are allowed to grow in an environment which is suitable to meet their social, emotional and educational needs. Children have to be priority item in the country's development agenda. They are the greatest gift of the humanity and they are the representation for the beautiful creation of God. Today's children are tomorrow's nation builders. However, it is an undisputable truth that we are not caring our children at their tender age (Lukose, 2012:217). Child is an organic cell of the society. The great poet Milton said, "child shows the man as morning shows the day". The name of the child is not tomorrow, but his name is 'today'. Children are the future custodian and torch bearers of the society. They are the messengers of our knowledge. Protection of children from all forms of abuse and exploitation across the world is the need of the hour. It is the most important obligation of the State to nourish them since their conception and birth in nurseries of the State equally, to whatever families high or low they belong. The feeling of high and low must be buried from the very birth of theirs (Batra, 2003:8).

Children are recipients of welfare measures. It was only during the twentieth century that the concept of children's rights emerged. This shift in focus the welfare to rights approach is significant. The rights approach is primarily concerned with issues of social justice, non-discrimination, equity and empowerment (Bajpai, 2004:1). The rights perspective is embodied in the United Nations Convention on the Rights of the Child 1989, which was ratified by India in 1992, guarantees the freedom from non-discrimination, uphold the best interest of the child, right to life, survival and development, right to protection and right to education which makes all other rights realizable and meaningful. This Convention recognised the right of every child to a standard of living adequate for the child's physical, mental, spiritual, moral and social development.

India's Integrated Child Development Services (ICDS) programme is the largest national programme for promoting the health and development of mothers and their children. The scheme is targeted at children below the age of six years and their mothers (particularly if they are pregnant and lactating) and the benefits take the form of *inter alia* supplementary nutrition, immunisation, regular heath checkup, education on nutrition and health and preschool learning. The scheme — based on the principle that the overall impact of these benefits would be greater if they were provided in an integrated manner, rather than on a piecemeal basis — is administered from *anganwadi* centre (AWCs) by workers and their helpers, who are trained and paid an honorarium (Kapil and Pradhan, 1999:21). Following a Supreme Court Directive, the Government have universalised the ICDS by sanctioning 14 lakh *anganwadi* centres.

Under nutrition remains a major threat to the survival, growth and development of Indian children. India's latest National Family Health Survey find that 43 per cent of Indian children 0-59 months old are underweight, with a weight for age below minus two standard deviations of the media weight-for-age in the World Health Organization (WHO, 2006a).Therefore, the challenge ahead for India is to ensure that national nutrition policies and social transformation are aimed at reducing inequalities and the disproportionate impact of under nutrition among the poorest and most vulnerable group in society.

India is signatory to the Millennium Development Goals (MDGs). The fourth MDG (MDG4) requires each countries to reduce by 2015 the under five child mortality rate by two-thirds in comparison to the level prevailing in 1990. For India, this translates into achieving an under five child mortality rate of 42 per 1,000 live births by 2015 (the 1990 rate being 125) (*The Hindustan Times*, 2014:6). Attaining the MDG4 would mean survival of millions of our children. India's success would also drive the world closer to the global MDG4.

United Nations Children' Fund (UNICEF) considers child protection as the prevention of or responding to the incidence of abuse, exploitation, violence and neglect of children. This includes commercial sexual exploitation, trafficking, child labour and harmful traditional practices, such as female genital mutilation/cutting and child marriage. Protection also allows children to have access to their other rights of survival, development, growth and participation. UNICEF maintains that when child protection fails or is absent children have a higher risk of death, poor physical and mental health, HIV/AIDS infection, educational problems, displacement, homelessness, vagrancy and poor parenting skills later in life.

The Government of India had adopted National Policy for Children in the year 1947. Our Constitution Makers, wise and sagacious as they were, had known that India of their vision would not be a reality if the children of the country are not nurtured and educated. The Constitution of India recognises the vulnerable position of children and their right to protection. It guarantees in Article 15, special attention to children through necessary and special laws and policies that safeguard their rights (Anuja, 2013:117). The data on missing children placed in Parliament in 2014 showed that more than 3.25 lakh children went missing between 2011 and 2014 (till June 2014), with an average of nearly 1 lakh kids disappearing every year. Among those missing 45 per cent of them remained untraceable, 55 per cent were girls. Maharashtra is among the worst States with over 50,000 kids having disappeared in the period; Madhya Pradesh, Delhi and Andhra Pradesh are distant competitors, each recording a figure of less than 25,000 (*The Times of India*, 2015:11).

Children are highly sensitive and are dependent on elders in their crucial early years. On the contrary, the caretakers often turn to be the predators of children. The World Health Organization's (WHO) 2002 report reveals that 150 million girl children and 73 million boys experience some forms of forced sexual intercourses or violence. It is our duty to see that rights of the children survive and thrive under umbrella of our adequate legal system. It is necessary to further sensitize the society, the public, the nation, NGOs and policy-makers. The society should ensure that their future should be shaped in harmony and cooperation. Children are amongst the most vulnerable members of our society, but are denied basic civil rights, perhaps most fundamentally the right to participate in decisions affecting them.

The Government shall endeavour that adequate resources are provided for child welfare programme and appropriate schemes are undertaken. At the same time, voluntary organisations engaged in the field of child welfare will continue to have the opportunity to develop, either on their own or with state assistance, in the field of education, health, recreation and social welfare services. The Government of India should also call upon the citizen and voluntary organisation to pay their part in the overall effort to attain the all-round development of children. Government should give free hand to National Commission for Protection of Child Rights (NCPCR) so that it can work effectively.

The book is divided into thirteen chapters. **Chapter one** makes a critical analysis of child sexual abuse. It is a critical pattern of crime which, if not dealt appropriately, the interest of the child will be at jeopardy. The perpetrator can be anyone who exploits the child vulnerability to gain sexual gratification. Sexual abuse can itself have dire long-term negative psychological consequences for its victims, but the degree of psychic trauma is as much and perhaps more dependent on the way the child victim is treated after disclosure than at the time of the offence itself. One of the most pervasive assumptions is that violence against children breeds violent adults.

Chapter two precisely attempts to highlight the problems of child labour. Protection of children from all forms of exploitation across the world is the need of the hour. Unfortunately, millions of children are deprived of their childhood and thereby they are subjected to exploitation.

The problem of child labour is one amongst the serious abuse of the children. Most of the rural children are employed in agricultural sector whereas in urban areas they are employed mainly in the unorganised sectors and most of them are bread winners, not the workers at leisure.

Chapter three examines the rights of children and the existing laws. Children were recipients of welfare measures. It is only during the twentieth century that the concept of children's rights emerged. This shift in focus from the 'welfare' to the 'rights' approach is signified. Rights are entitlements. The rights perspective is embodied in the United Nations Convention on the Rights of the Child 1989, which is landmark in international human rights legislation. India ratified the Convention on the Rights of the Child in December 1992.

Chapter four highlights the Mid-Day Meal Scheme in Bihar. With the objective of improving health and education of the poor children, India has started Mid-Day Meal Scheme in the Government and Government assisted primary schools. The administrative and logistical responsibilities of this scheme are enormous and, therefore, offering food stamps or income transfer to targeted recipients is considered as an alternative. In this chapter Bihar Mid-Day Meal Scheme is evaluated, in Gandaman-Dharmsati Village under Mashrakh Block at Chapra in Bihar, Saran District, where 23 children lost their life after eating sub-standard food with poisonous pesticide. The quality of mid-day meals served under the scheme has been a cause of concern for a long time in the State.

Chapter five seeks to focus on the girls' stalking, which is related to harassment and intimidation and may include following the victim in person or monitoring them. Stalking is a pattern of repeated and unwanted attention, harassment, contact, or any other course of conduct directed at a specific person that would cause a reasonable person to feel fear. This chapter also focuses on cyberstalking. Cyberstalking shares important characteristics with offline stalking; many stalkers — online or offline — are motivated by a desire to control their victims. In the case of online harassment, the difficulties of tracing the cyberstalker is most complicated issue as the stalker remains anonymous and problems of dealing with harassment crosses national boundaries.

Chapter six picks up a lively debate on the issue of child pornography. The internet has increased the range, volume and accessibility of sexually abusive imagery, including child pornography. This chapter examines the circulation and typology of online child pornography offending, as well as law enforcement responses to this problem. Child pornography is the evidence of the sexual abuse of a child and the production of child pornography always presupposes a crime committed towards the child. It objectifies and degrades children. It may be used by abusers as a means to manipulate a child.

Chapter seven focuses on female foeticide. It is the most disgraceful act on the part of human being who is considered to be the superior creatures of God responsible to create conducive conditions for the existence and survival of their fellows. The foetus contains life and its elimination is an awful crime. Coupled with prospective parents desperate for a boy child, and physicians who are carrying out these abortions, female foeticide has become a shameful and shocking reality of our nation. Foeticide can be seen everywhere in India, and it has become more common with the advent and easy availability of technology, such as amniocentesis and sonography, that enables the determination of the gender of the foetus. Despite Government measures and laws against it, foeticide has not seen a decrease in its rate; on the contrary, it is increasing rapidly.

Chapter eight deals with child marriage in Indian society. Prejudices were also responsible for the origin of child marriage. By getting married as a child, she is denied her basic right to be a child and enjoy her childhood, as her brother do. The very experience of being uprooted from her parental home and going to live in her-in-law house is a traumatic experience, as various kinds of duties, obligations's, negations are imposed on her, which causes strain and frustration in her personality. Marriage at an early age, denies children, the opportunities to have education, training and income-generating skills and creates difficulties in their way in attaining maturity, self-confidence and an all-round development of personality.

Chapter nine highlights the horrific massacring young and innocent girls daring to choose their life-partners much against the accepted social norms by the allegedly cast group/*Khap* panchayat; the culture of regulating and controlling their conduct and life and amputating, shattering the personalities marching against the accepted patriarchal traditions in the guise of protecting the family or caste. This chapter also suggests steps which can be adopted by lawmakers, enforcement agencies for checking the cruel practice of victimising the young girls for protecting and restoring the notion of honour.

Chapter ten delves deep into the vital issue of child rape. It is not only a crime against the girl child (victims), it is a crime against the entire society. It destroys the entire psychology of a girl child and pushes her into deep emotional crises. It is only by her sheer will power that she rehabilitates herself in the society which, on coming to know of the rape, looks down upon her in derision and contempt. To many feminist and psychiatrists, rape is less a sexual offence than an act of aggression aimed at degrading and humiliating girls. What we require are reforms in the police and greater gender sensitisation among the force as well as within the judicial system.

Chapter eleven argues quite convincingly that women are facing violence for no other reason than that they are women. Recently in India, acid attacks have also emerged out as a form of gender based violence aimed at silencing and controlling women and young girls. Acid attacks are often directed at those women and young girls who reject the advances of men as if they have no right and liberty for rejection in the male dominated society. The perpetrators are familiar with the nature, habits and movement of girls and women on whom they intend to seek revenge and are, therefore, able to plan the attack in advance. The act rarely kills but causes severe physical, psychological and social scarring. The Penal provisions against perpetrators in India have now been strengthened, but the question of eliminating easy access to acid has received little attention. This chapter highlights the pathetic condition of victims who are leading dejected life aftermath of acid attack.

Chapter twelve examines child's education which is one of the important factors for development and emancipation. If a child is nurtured and groomed properly by imparting him not just good but best school education, it is not only the child alone who groom into a mature personality, but it is also the entire society which gains. The Constitution of India with respect to education provides a *Triveni Sangam* — the right of person, duty of the citizens and the obligation of the State. The Constitution of India mandates the State to provide free and compulsory good quality elementary education to all children up to the age of 14. This chapter also highlights the Right of Children to Free and Compulsory Education Act 2009.

Chapter thirteen discusses the trafficking in child for prostitution. Trafficking in children is one of the worst and most brazen abuses violating the rights of child. It is a blot on our collective consciousness. There are violations in various ways of the basic rights of children but nothing is more horrendous than exploiting them sexually and engaging them in prostitution. Using children to satisfy an adult's sexual needs is something so cruel and mean that it does not exist in an animal kingdom.

Children in prostitution are pathetic victims of power and cruelty in a male dominated society and greed driven economy.

REFERENCES

Aguayo Victor, Gayatri Singh, Nina Badgaiyan, 2014. "Scoring Child Nutrition in India", *Economic and Political Weekly*, April 5, Vol. XLIX, No. 14.

Anuja, S., 2013. "Human Rights of Street Children to Safe and Healthy Childhood — The Approach and Challenges", *Indian Bar Review*, Vol. XL(4).

Bajpai, Asha, 2004. *Child Rights in India: Law, Policy and Practice*, Oxford University Press, New Delhi.

Batra, A.P., 2008. "Crime Against Children", *Nayaya Deep*, Vol. IX, Issue 4, October.

Batra, Manjula, 2003. *Women and Law and Law Relating to Children in India*, Allahabad Law Agency, Haryana.

Choudhary, Baidyanath, 2004. "Law's Concern on Children — On International and National Standard", in Nirmal Kanti Chakrabarti (ed), *Law and Child*, R. Cambray & Co. Private Ltd., Kolkata.

Choudhary, Renuka, 2006. "ICDS: India's Response to Early Child Development", *Yojana*, November, pp. 5-9.

Debabrata, Roma, 1997. *The Lost Childhood*, National Commission for Women, New Delhi.

Encyclopaedia Britannica. Encyclopaedia Britannica Inc. Chicago, 2007, 15th Ed., Vol. 16, p.19.

Gautam, Manjulika, 2006. "Child Development in India", *Yojana*, November, pp. 25-29.

Kapil, U. and R. Pradhan, 1999. "Integrated Child Development Services Scheme (ICDS) and its Impact on the Nutritional Status of Children", *Indian Journal of Public Health*, 43(1), pp. 21-25.

Konin, Lingaraj, M., 2013. "Child Labour — A Social-Legal Empirical Appraisal", *Indian Bar Review*, Vol. XL(1).

Lukose, Lisa, P., 2012. "Sexual Abuse of Children: Coarse Sacrilege of Human Rights", *Indian Bar Review*, Vol. XXXIX(4).

The Hindustan Times, 2014. "So Many Young Lives to Save", June 16, Kolkata, p. 6.

The Times of India, 2015. "Centre Casual about Missing Children: SC", April 18, Kolkata, p. 11.

WHO, 2006a. "Assessment of Difference in Linear Growth among Populations in the World Health Organisation Multi-centre Growth Reference Study", *Acta Paediatrica Suppl.*, 450, pp. 56-65.

WHO, 2006a. "WHO Child Growth Standards Based on Length/Height, Weight and Age", *Acta Paediatrica Suppl.*, 450, pp. 76-85.

1

CHILD ABUSE: Violation of Human Rights

"Most of the Indian children are condemned to live in culture based on denial, neglect, indifference and downright cruelty and exploitation in many cases. Most of our children do not, in real terms have the opportunity to enjoy and experience childhood. The denial of their very human rights leads to a thwarting of their personalities, distorting their dignified march towards adulthood."

INSAF, Commission on Children

Introduction

Children are considered as future of a country and are supremely important asset. Their nurture and solitude are our responsibility, but in our society their basic rights has been violated. All basic rights which are considered as human rights are applicable to all boys and girls who are under 18 years age group. It may be so that society may differ in their ideas on childhood and child personality development but it is accepted notion that children need special care and protection for healthy development of their personality as they are considered as vulnerable section of society. Special instruments have been drawn up to safeguard and enforce child rights. The *UN Convention on the Rights of the Child* (CRC) drawn up in 1989 and has been ratified by almost all member nations. The rights of the child as defined by the CRC Convention includes equality like adults, children can be subjected to discrimination which has a negative impact on a child's opportunities and condition in life. Therefore, all children are entitled to equal right and Governments have an obligation to uphold these. Every child has a right to develop to his or her potential and is entitled to right of basic needs, right to free primary education, right to protection from economic exploitation and right to special assistance for children with special needs. Sexual abuse of child is a fundamental violation of the rights of children. It is shameful and shocking that the person who is supposed to be responsible for socialisation of the children is the one who are destroying their future. Childhood, which ideally should be a carefree time of life filled with love and joy, becomes an ugly and frustrated experience for abused children.

Child sexual abuse is defined as any kind of physical or mental violation of child with a sexual intent, usually by an elder person who is in possession of trust or power *vis-à-vis* the child. It is not confined within family and household. The perpetrator can be anyone who exploits the child vulnerability to gain sexual gratification. The anthropological definition of incest (defined as a sexual act imposed on a child or adolescent by any person within the family constellation) focuses on the consanguinity of the individual in the relationship and the nature of sexual act, which must include sexual intercourse. This has limitations in that much sexual abuse is conducted within the family structure without there necessarily being a blood relationship. This is primarily so in the case of stepfathers, the mother's sexual partner or boyfriend, friends of the family, or close neighbours. The abused child in the presence of such family constellations often has the same emotional investment and dependency needs as the child who is incestuously abused by father, grandfather or brother. The legal definition of incest is exclusively on penile penetration and sexual intercourse and ignores the full range of sexually abusive acts that have been reported, which nevertheless violate the child's boundaries and includes full intercourse, but does incorporates non-touching behaviour as well as physical contact behaviours. The non-touching behaviours includes exhibitionism, voyeurism, nudity, verbal innuendos, genital exposure, and the use of pornography. Physical behaviour includes fondling of the breast or genital area of the child, kissing, fellatio, cunnilingus, digital penetration of the anus, sodomy, dry intercourse in which the abuser rubs his penis against the child's genital area, inner thighs or buttocks. Child sexual abuse is, therefore, defined as the involvement of dependent child or adolescent in sexual activities with an adult in which the child is used as a sexual object for gratification of the older person's needs or desire, and to which the child is unable to give consent due to the unequal power in the relationship.

The definition of sexual abuse of children is best understood when problem is related to pedophilia. The basis of sexual exploitation of children is pedophilia — sexual attraction to children. Pedophilia is the attraction to or love of (philia) children (ped). A 'pedophile' is an adult that is sexually attracted to children. United Nations have also defined child sexual abuse as contacts or interaction between a child and an older or more knowledgeable child or adult (a stranger, sibling, or person in a position of authority, such as a parent or a caretaker) when the child is being used as an object of gratification for the older child's or adult sexual needs. These contacts or interactions are carried out against the child, using force, trickery, bribes, threats or pressure (UNICEF, 2001).

FORMS OF CHILD ABUSE

Child abuse can take various forms, namely commercial sexual abuse, emotional, physical, sexual abuse and neglect.

Commercial Sexual Abuse

Commercial sexual abuse prevailed in the form of child labour and child prostitution. It is oldest oppression for child. Child labour includes all forms of slavery or practices similar to slavery, such as the sale and trafficking of children, debt bondage and serfdom and forced or compulsory labour, and use, procuring or offering of child for prostitution, for the production of pornography or for pornographic performance. Child prostitution in India is closely linked with the poverty and helplessness of those parents who cannot afford for the proper care and protection of their minor children. It has been proved that majority of teenagers who enter into the profession usually come from lower-class homes. Sometimes, children are inducted forcibly through abduction, trafficking and deceit.

Sexual Abuse

It can be mentioned of four types, namely exposure which is viewing of sexual acts and exhibition, molestation, sexual intercourse on a chronic basis and rape in which there is acute assault intercourse. Rape can be of two kind — first one is intra-familial and extra-familial, i.e. rape by known person or person in authority and rape by stranger. Child rape is a great social stigma and it shows complete degeneration of moral values in society. In some cases the victims of rape are not even accepted at home. Victim is either too traumatised by the experience or the parents, out of concern for child future, hush up the matter. The rapist knows that there are high chance of his outrage against minor not being discovered. This acts as a major motivating factors, many victims do not go to the police out of fear of adverse publicity and unnecessary harassment. Apart from the delay or even absence of justice, the victims have to face similar incidence every now and then. When the victims do not find any safe place in society and do not see any future prospects, they enter into the den of prostitution.

Neglect

Neglect is probably the hardest type of abuse to define. It occurs when a child does not have adequate food, housing, cloth, medical care or supervision. Emotional neglect happens when a parent does not provide enough emotional support or deliberately and consistently pays very little or no attention to a child. Neglect can be physical, educational, emotional and medical. Physical neglect includes refusal or delay in seeking health care, abandonment, expulsion from home. Educational neglect includes the allowance of chronic failure to enroll a child of mandatory school age in school, and failure to attend to a special educational need. Medical neglect includes failure to provide necessary medical or mental treatment.

Emotional Abuse

It can be defined as acts or omission by the parents or the other caregivers that have caused, or could cause, serious behavioural, cognitive emotional or mental disorder. It is an attack on a child's emotional and social development and is a basic threat to healthy human development. It is like brain washing in that it systematically wears away at the victim's self-confidence, sense of self-worth, trust in their own perception and self-concept. Emotional abuse and neglect are at the core of all types of child maltreatment and have the most harmful effects on the physical and psychological development and well-being of children. Emotional Abuse can be discussed in the form of rejecting, ignoring, isolating, harassment and so on.

Rejecting

Parents who lack the ability to bond will often display rejecting behaviour towards a child. They tell a child in a variety of ways that he or she is unwanted. They may also tell the child to leave, call his or her names and tell the child he or she is worthless. They may not talk to or hold the young child as he or she grows. The child may become the family scapegoat, being blamed for all the family's problem.

Ignoring

Ignoring a child deprives the child of all the essential stimulation and interaction necessary for emotional, intellectual and social development, for example parents may not show attachment to the child or provide nurturance. They may show no interest in the child, express affection or even recognise the child's presence. Many times the parents are physically there but emotionally unavailable.

Isolating

A parent who abuses a child through isolation may not allow the child to engage in appropriate activities with his or her peers, may keep a baby in his or her room, not exposed to stimulation or may prevent teenagers from participating in extracurricular activities. Parents may require the child to stay in his or her room from the time school lets out until the next morning, or restrict eating to isolation or seclusion.

Harassment

It scares the child and repeated exposure to fear can alter the child physically, lowering their ability to deal with other stressful situations. Repeated evocations of the stress response alter the child physically, lowering their ability to fight off disease, increasing their risk for many stress related ailments. Aside from the physical effects, a child living in terror has no opportunity to develop anything other than unhealthy and anti-social survival skill and character.

Coldness

Children learn to interact with the world through their early interactions with their parents. If parents are warm and loving, children grow to see the world as a secure place for exploration and learning. When parents are cold to their children, they deprive the child of necessary ingredients for intellectual and social development. Children, who are subjected to consistent coldness grow to see the world as a cold, uninviting place, and will likely have seriously impaired relationships in the future. They may also never feel confident to explore and learn.

Physical Abuse

Physical Abuse is physical injury (raging from minor bruises to severe fracture or death) as a result of punching, beating, kicking, hitting, shaking, throwing, stabbing, biting, burning or otherwise harming a child. The parent or caretaker may not have intended to hurt the child. It may, however, be the result of over-discipline or physical punishment that is inappropriate to the child's age.

Child Marriage

Child marriage is a form of sexual abuse of children. Child brides or the bridegroom do not understand the solemnity of marriage ceremonies, but for adult person it is safest way of keeping property and money within the family and of preserving the chastity of their daughters. Early marriage is a form of sexual abuse of the girls' child as they have to become mother. Early motherhood deprives the girls an opportunity for development and schooling, they are made to assume domestic and child care responsibility which hamper their intellectual and personality development.

IMPACT OF CHILD ABUSE

The impact of child abuse is often discussed in physical, psychological, behavioural and societal terms.

Physical Consequences

Physical abuse concerns the violent shaking of baby. Shaking baby syndrome can cause vomiting, respiratory distress, seizures and death. Impaired brain development can cause important region of the brain to fail to form properly. This abuse can result in infections, bruises, broken bones, visual and auditory impairment, brain damage, burns and deaths. Physically abused children have also been found to be move likely to interpret the actions of their peers as hostile, and to respond inappropriately in an aggressive manner. In case of chronic abuse, the stress may result in impaired brain development and various resultant disabilities like physical deformities, proneness to stress disorder, conduct disorder, hyper activity, sleep disturbance and so on. Poor physical health can persist throughout life.

Psychological Consequences

Abused children have been found to display relationship problems with their parents and peers. For instance, they may be anxious or ambivalent towards their parents and be more passive and withdrawn with their peers. Abused child is associated with intellectual deficits and other academic problem such as delay in acquiring language and so on. They also have high rates of mental disorders like depression, anxiety, eating disorder, Post Traumatic Stress Disorder (PTSD), self-injury behaviour, suicide attempts and alcohol dependency increases. Child rape has both initial effect and long-term effect. In the initial effect, the emotional reactions are of fear, anger, hostility, guilt and shame. The long-term effects are worse as the child goes through the stage of depression, self-destruction, anxiety and tension. Victims are totally isolated, stigmatised and suffer from a negative self-concept.

Behavioural Consequence

Abused and neglected children may lead to low academic achievement, poor concentration, personality disorder and other problems like delinquency, teen pregnancy, drug abuse and health problems. Emotional abuse and neglect increased the likelihood of adult criminal behaviour. In some chronic cases it may lead to sexual dysfunction, or even to child prostitution. Neglected children are likely to smoke cigarettes, consume alcohol or take illicit drug. As many as two-third of people in drug treatment programmes reported being abused as children. Abusive parents often have experienced abuse during their own childhoods. It is estimated that approximate one-third of abused and neglected children would eventually be victimised by their parents.

Societal Consequences

Society is affected indirectly and directly by child abuse (sexual, emotional, and neglect). Indirect effect includes long-term economic consequences such as juvenile and adult criminal activities, mental illness and personality disorder. Direct effect includes those associated with maintaining a child welfare system to investigate and provide interventions for abused and neglected children. Most emotionally abused and neglected children feel isolated as they have little confidence in others. They also fear of lose of control in relationship with peers and generally fail to develop trustworthy and intimate relation with peers and adults.

LEGAL MEASURES AND IMPLICATIONS

The first significant advance in establishing a broad conception of Children's right under international law was the *Declaration of Geneva adopted by League of Nations in 1924.* The Declaration has been described as a landmark shifting contrast to earlier and more narrowly focused treaties dealing with trafficking and child labour. The Declaration contains five principles for the protection and care of children. Under Article 4 the fundamental principle was declared that *the child must be protected against every form of exploitation*. Because of their immaturity and fragility children need a "particular protection" as determined by the International Declaration of the Rights of the Child, accepted on 20 November, 1959 by the Assembly of the United Nations.

The 1959 *Declaration on the Rights of the Child* proclaimed that the child shall be protected against all forms of neglect, cruelty, and exploitation. The child shall not be the subject of traffic in any form. The member states of the United Nations, convinced that the exploitation of children is of paramount concern, set forth to establish procedures that protected children against continuing and evolving violations to their rights. On 20 November, 1989, the General Assembly of the United Nations unanimously adopted the *Convention on the Rights of the Child*.

Then the World Conference on Human Rights, 14-25 June, 1993, Vienna, Austria, took new steps to promote and protect the rights of women and children by supporting the creation of new mechanisms and advocating the universal ratification of the Convention on the Rights of the Child by the year 1995. In August 1996, at the First World Congress, the representatives from 122 countries including India adopted the *Stockholm Declaration and Agenda for Action Against Commercial Sexual Exploitation of Children and Child Sex Tourism and Pornography*. This declaration proposes actions to be taken at the national and local levels towards prevention, protection and recovery/reintegration and child participation with respect to commercial sexual exploitation of children.

In December 2001, *the Second World Congress against Commercial Sexual Exploitation of Children* was hosted by the Government of Japan at Yokohama. The objective of the Congress was to review the progress in implementing the Agenda for Action adopted in Stockholm and to strengthen action to eradicate commercial sexual exploitation of children.

The Constitution of India under directive principles of state policy contains provisions for protection of children. Article 39(e) says that it is the duty of state to secure that children of tender age are not abused and forced by economic necessity to enter vocations unsuited to their age and strength. Article 39(f) ensures that children are given opportunities and facilities to develop in healthy manner and in condition of freedom and dignity. Article 23 prohibits trafficking of women for immoral purposes. The Constitution directs the states to enact special legislation and policies for protecting children and youth against exploitation of usual and material abandonment.

Though there is no comprehensive law to deal with the cases of child sexual abuse but the Indian Penal Code, 1860 shows the provisions to deal with child sexual abuse under Sections 354, 366A, 366B, 375, 376 and 377. Section 375 deals with rape and 376 provide punishment for rape which shall not be less than seven years. Section 354 says that whoever assaults or uses criminal force to any woman, intending to outrage or knowing it to be likely that he will thereby outrage her modesty, shall be punished with imprisonment of either description for a term which may extend to two years or with fine or with both. The other provisions of IPC, which are invoked, are related to unnatural practices like Section 377. This is generally invoked when boy children are sexually abused.

The Suppression of Immoral Trafficking Act 1986 under Section 8 provides protection to both boys and girls from sexual abuse. Under Section 67 of the Information Technology Act, 2000 publication and transmission of pornography is an offence. The Child Marriage Restraint (Amendment) Act 1978 lays down the minimum age for marriage. It is now eighteen years for girls and twenty one years for boys. There are still thousands of child marriages reported throughout the country. Early marriages are a form of child sexual abuse and a violation of a child's freedom to enjoy childhood. The Protection of Children from Sexual Offences Act 2012 (POCSO) is a landmark legislation as it is the first law enacted, which exclusively addresses the issue of child sexual abuse in India.

Judicial Intervention to Protect the Children from Sexual Abuse

Judiciary too has played an important role in curbing the menace of child sexual abuse. A woman's modesty is her sex whoever uses criminal force with intent to outrage it commits an offence under Section 354 of IPC. In *State of Punjab* vs. *Major Singh* AIR, 1967 where judiciary for the first time highlighted the concept of abuse by outraging the modesty of a woman. In this case a female child of seven and half months was considered to be a woman under this section as the accused had outraged and intended to outrage, whatever modesty the little victim was capable of. The accused had walked into the room where the child was sleeping and committed an indecent assault on her. In the case of *Gorakh Daji Ghadge* vs. *The State of Maharashtra* Cr.L.J. 1980, where the father has raped his thirteen years old daughter in his home. The High Court stated that crimes in which women are victims need to be severely dealt with and in extreme cases such as this when the accused, who is the father of the victim girl has thought it fit to "deflower" his own daughter of tender age to gratify his lust, then only a deterrent sentence can meet at the end of justice.

The need for a law on child sexual abuse was brought to the attention of the Supreme Court in the case of *Sakshi* vs. *Union of India and Others* AIR 1999. The petitioner submitted that the expression 'sexual intercourse' as contained in Section 375 of the IPC should include all forms of penetration as the restrictive interpretative of penetration as existing in Section 375 defeated the very purpose and intent of the provision for punishment for rape under Section 376. The IPC, the Indian Evidence Act and the Criminal Procedure Code should be accordingly amended. Pursuant to the order passed by the Supreme Court in this matter, the Law Commission of India reviewed the laws related to child sexual abuse and recommended amendments to Indian Penal Code in its 172nd report.

The Supreme Court in the case of *Vishaal Jeet* vs. *Union of India* AIR 1990, issued directions to the State Government for eradicating child prostitution and setting up rehabilitative homes for those children. In the infamous *Freddy Peats* case where Freddy Peat was running a racket in child sex abuse for years, maintained destitute children in his orphanage in order to offer them to the European Sex Tourist who regularly came to Goa to have sex with these children. The case was handled by Sheela Barse the child right activist whose intervention in this case led to child friendly procedures by the trial court. They are as follows:

- Trial was held in camera in the Chamber of the Session's Judge. Similarly, examinations of child victims/witnesses were also conducted in camera, so that, the witnesses are not awed by the court atmosphere.
- All persons in the trial were in informal dress.
- No police officer was present inside the chamber or at the place where the trial was conducted.
- While recording evidence, the child was directed to face the judge so that he will not have occasion to look at the accused and be frightened.

After the *Freddy Peat's case* where Supreme Court awarded 20 years rigorous imprisonment, the Indian Judiciary once again made the pedophiles realised all over the world that *India is not the destination for sex tourism in future*. The Additional Session's Judge P.S. Paranjape of Mumbai on 18th March, 2006 convicted the UK National Duncan Grant and U.S. National Allen Waters to six years rigorous imprisonment for sexually exploiting the children of Orphanage (Anchorage) at Colaba, Cuffe Parade and Murud Janjira. Both Grant and Waters were deported to India in June 2005 as they had fled from the country after committing the offence in September 2004. They were guilty under IPC Section 377 (unnatural intercourse), Section 373 (buying minors for the purpose of prostitution), Section 372 (selling minors for the purpose of prostitution), and Section 23 of the Juvenile Justice Act.

Conclusion

The child sexual abuse not only has damaging and long-term impact on victims, but also affects the families, communities and society. Victims suffer several trauma or damage which can be emotional, physical and mental. Psychological problems may last a lifetime if the process of healing does not take place. Health related problems like Sexually Transmitted Disease (STD), Acquired Immune Deficiency Syndrome (AIDS) at an early age can be some of the disastrous outcome of child abuse when it takes the form of commercial sexual exploitation. With the family emotional support system getting destroyed, victims face social isolation and they may feel lonely and frightened.

Techniques for interviewing child victims of sexual abuse need to be developed. There is still much to be done to reduce the difficult experiences in the courts. The courts have shown inconsistency in dealing with child rape cases. Procedural innovation such as exception to rule of hearsay, use of expert testimony, mandatory reporting laws, delayed discovery statutes, expeditious hearing, an appointment of guardian *ad litem* need to be introduced. Recommendations of the 172nd Law Commission Report of Ministry of Law, Justice and Company Affairs should be accepted and Indian Penal Code, Indian Evidence Act and the Criminal Procedure Code should be accordingly amended to ensure successful prosecution in case of child sexual abuse and to protect the best interest of child. The Indian Judiciary also have to take bold steps in combating the menace of child sexual abuse as it took in the *Duncan Grant and Allen Waters case.*

REFERENCES

Agnes, Flavia, 2001. *Law and Gender Inequality*, Oxford University Press, New Delhi.
Bajpai, Asha, 2003. *Child Rights in India*, Oxford University Press, New Delhi.
Baligar, Vinaya and Prabha, V., 1999. *Mother and Girl Child*, Rawat Publications, New Delhi.
Chandra, Sudhir, 1998. *Enslaved Daughter*, Oxford University Press, New Delhi.
D'souza, Engene, 2002. *Crime and Social Justice*, Commonwealth Publisher, New Delhi.
Dutta, Abhijit, 2002. *Child Marriage an Adult Obsession*, Minerva Associates, Kolkata.
Goldstein, Seth, L., 1999. *The Sexual Exploitation of Children*, New York: CRC Press LLC.
Joshi, Madhu, 1997. *Women and Children in Prostitution — Human Right Perspective*, Joint Women Programme, New Delhi.
Krause, Harry D., 1992. *Child Law*, New York University Press, New York.
Krishna, S., 1996. *Restoring Childhood — The Commonwealth Human Right Initiative*, Konark Publishers Pvt. Ltd., New Delhi.
Miles, Angela, R.; Finn, Geraldine, 2002. *Feminism from Pressure to Politics*, Rawat Publications, New Delhi.
Mishra, Lakshmidhar, 2000. *Child Labour in India*, Oxford University Press, New Delhi.
Rao, Mamta, 2005. *Women and Children*, Eastern Book Company, New Delhi.
Sherwani, A., 1998. *The Girl Child Crisis*, India Social Institute, New Delhi.

Legislation

Convention on the Rights of the Child (CRC) 1989
Child Marriage Restraint Act 1928
Criminal Procedure Code 1973
Dowry Prohibition Act 1961
Indian Penal Code 1860
Second World Congress Against Commercial Sexual Exploitation of Children.
Stockholm Declaration and Agenda for Action Against Commercial Sexual Exploitation of Children and Child Sex Tourism and Pornography.
The Indian Evidence Act 1872

2

CHILD LABOUR:
Ultimate Denial of Child's Rights

"I am a child,
All the world waits for my, coming,
All the earth watches with interest to see, what I shall become,
Civilization hangs in the balance,
For what I am, the world of tomorrow will be,
I am child,
You hold in your hand my destiny.
You determine largely whether I shall succeed or fail,
Give me, I pray you, these things that makes for happiness
Train me, I beg you that I may be blessing to the world".

M.C. Mehta *vs.* State of Tamil Nadu & Others (AIR 1997 SC 699)

Introduction

Child labour is generally speaking, work for children that harms them or exploits them in someway (physically, morally, or by blocking access to education). It denotes the use of a child below the age of fourteen for any kind of labour or employment in exchange of wages or other forms of monetary gratification. Child labour has been one of the worst and most widespread forms of violation of human rights that one could see all over the globe. In theory, child labour does not exist in most countries, for most nations do not admit its existence in their realms. In truth, however, the magnitude of child labour both — overt and covert — is found around the world today and particularly in Third World countries like India, Pakistan, Bangladesh or Nepal is awesome. But nowhere child labour is more conspicuous and in less deplorable a condition than in our country. In India, the problem of child labour is inextricably linked to certain basic social problems that we have been grappling with over the past five decades of freedom: Illiteracy, unemployment and poverty.

A 2003 survey by the International Labour Organization suggested that there are 246 million child labourers (aged 14 or less) in the world, and that as many as 180 million of them are engaged in hazardous activities that put them at direct physical risk. India has the largest number of child labourers in the world. The United Nations Children's Fund (UNICEF) estimates that there are more than 35 million such children, accounting for 14 per cent of the children in the 5-14 age group. Other unofficial estimates are much higher, ranging between 60 and 125 million child labourers. According to the Labour Ministry's estimation, Uttar Pradesh has the largest number of child workers in the country — 19 lakhs in the 5-14 age groups. The evaluation essentially covers the carpet and silk weaving industry of the Mirzapur-Varanasi belt, the lock and key manufacturing units of Aligarh, the brass vessel industry of Moradabad, the sports goods units of Meerut, the fireworks production units of Jhansi and the brick kilns spread across the State. Unofficial and other estimates of social activists cover 30 lakhs. It is interesting to note that the four States that account for more than 40 per cent of all the officially recorded child labour in India — Andhra Pradesh, Karnataka, Maharashtra and Tamil Nadu are among the richer states in India. Andhra Pradesh which had the dubious population of child labourers had bequeathed this honour to Uttar Pradesh. Table 2.1 below makes the comparison of the number of child labourers that has increased in some states and decreased in some states in respect of the Census of 1991 and that of 2001.

Table 2.1: Comparison of Child Labourers in Census 1991 and Census 2001

States/Union Territory	*Census 1991*	*Census 2001*
(1)	*(2)*	*(3)*
Andhra Pradesh	16,61,940	13,63,339
Assam	3,27,598	3,51,416
Bihar	9,42,245	11,17,500
Chhattisgarh	—	3,64,572
Gujarat	5,23,585	4,85,530
Haryana	1,09,691	2,53,491
Jammu & Kashmir	**	1,75,630
Karnataka	9,76,247	8,22,615
Madhya Pradesh	13,52,563	10,65,259
Maharashtra	10,68,418	7,64,075
Manipur	16,493	28,836
Jharkhand	—	4,07,200
Uttarakhand	—	70,183
Odisha	4,52,394	3,77,594

(Contd.)

Table 2.1 (*Contd.*)

(1)	*(2)*	*(3)*
Punjab	1,42,868	1,77,268
Rajasthan	7,74,199	12,62,570
Tamil Nadu	5,78,889	4,18,801
Uttar Pradesh	14,10,086	19,27,997
West Bengal	7,11,691	8,57,087
Delhi	27,351	41,899
Goa	4,656	4,138

Note: ** Census could not be conducted. Figures relate to workers of age-group 5-14 years.

Source: Registrar General & Census Commissioner of India.

Causes of Child Labour

One of the primary causes of child labour is poverty, this problem affects more than 80 per cent of rural families, across the globe, where there is no source of fixed income, except for agricultural and other resource, based professions. However, agriculture is a seasonal activity and although it employs a larger part of rural population. It is never considered as a continuous source of income.

Consequently, the parents forced to put their children into certain skilled professions in the hope of a continuous income. Such skilled work areas include weaving; plantation sorting, etc., although a large part of the rural child population is employed in unskilled labour like domestic help, and other low wages industrial employment. Certain identified causes which increase the scope of child labour are enumerated as follows:

Poverty: It has been identified as a primary cause that helps child labour to thrive across the globe. Although the problem mainly dominates the developing nations, where the per capita income is considerably low, even the developed world is not truly free from the same. More often than usual, in families where the per capita income is too low to maintain a minimum standard of living, parents forced their children to work for a minimum wage so that it adds up to the total income of the family.

Increase in Population: Families with more number of dependent members will obviously have a low per capita income. This in-turn induces child labour. More and more number of children are born which indicates that more number of children will bring increased income.

Rapid Urbanisation: This is an important factor which has induced child labour heavily. In the post-globalisation era, employment opportunities are enhanced due to the dominance of private operators in almost all the sectors. This has raised the per capita income specially of the middle class families and has resulted in these people shifting more and more towards urban areas where job opportunities are more. Moreover, rapid industrialisation has ushered in urbanisation and this has created a huge demand for domestic and industrial manpower.

Rise in Women Employment: This is yet another important factor which has largely increased child labour after the globalisation, liberalisation policies. Consequently, there has been a huge need for domestic help which was earlier provided by women and is now substituted by children. This is because they are easily available and ready to work for low wages and can also be exploited as per the will of their masters.

Failure of Government to Make Primary Education Services Accessible: This is especially applicable to rural areas where the primary educational institutions are located far away and do not have facilities of better accessibility. This induces the parents not to send their children to basic school specially the girl children due to long hours of travel and lack of security. They are then employed elsewhere to earn a supporting income for the family.

Religious and Other Reasons: Lack of education and awareness make rural people believe that children are gift of God and there is no harm in having them in large numbers. Having uncounted children without the future thought of child survival is also leading towards the problem of child labour.

Laws of Labour Enforcement and Restrictions: By labour enforcement laws and restrictions we mean Government policy objectives which should be curbed or made flexible as per the needs of the labour market.

CLASSIFICATION OF HAZARDS OF CHILD LABOUR

The hazards of child labour can be classified into three categories, which are —

1. ***Physical Hazards:*** There are jobs that are hazardous and affect child labourers immediately. They affect the overall health coordination, strength, vision and hearing of children. Working in mines, construction sites, carrying heavy loads are some of the activities that put children directly at risk physically.
2. ***Cognitive Hazards:*** Education helps a child to develop cognitively, emotionally and socially, and needless to say, education is often gravely reduced by child labour. Cognitive development includes literacy, numeracy and the acquisition of knowledge necessary

for normal life. Work may take much of the children's time that it becomes impossible to attend school and even if they do attend, they may be tired and less attentive to follow the lessons.

3. ***Emotional, Social and Moral Hazards:*** There are jobs that may jeopardise a child's psychological and social growth more than physical growth, for example domestic job can involve relatively light work. Long hours of work, the physical and the psychological abuse to which the child domestic labourers are exposed, make the work hazardous. Moral hazards generally refer to dangers arising from illegal activities which the children are forced to be engaged, such as trafficking of drugs.

LEGAL PROVISIONS

Child labour is a universally acknowledged problem with so un-proportionate and explosive dimensions that it had been a cause of serious concern since long and number of Acts, Regulations and Declarations had been made on this behalf. On the threshold of Independence when Constitution was drafted, the issue of child labour was addressed. Child labour is right against exploitation and this right is guaranteed by Articles 23 and 24 of the Constitution. Article 24 prohibits employment of children below the age of fourteen years in mines and shall not be engaged in other hazardous employment. Thus, there was no ban on employing children. Article 39(f) casts a duty upon the State to direct its policy towards securing that children are given opportunities and facilities to develop in a healthy manner and conditions of freedom and dignity and that childhood and youth are protected against exploitation and against moral and material abandonment, infringement of fundamental right guaranteed by Article 24. Article 39(e) lays that the health and strength of workers, men and women and the tender age of children are not abused and that citizens are not forced by economic necessity to enter avocations unsuited to their age or strength. Article 47 states the responsibility of the State to raise the nutritional levels, and standard of living of its citizens and to improve public health. Article 45 directed the State to provide free and compulsory primary education for all children until they completed the age of fourteen years. This was to be done within 10 years of the commencement of the Constitution but unfortunately the Government could not fulfil this Constitutional commitment. Article 45 was substituted in 2002 (Eighty-sixth Amendment Act) when the right to free and compulsory education was made a fundamental right under Article 21-A. Article 45 now provides that the State shall endeavour to provide early childhood care and education for all children until they complete the age of six years.

While Child Labour (Prohibition and Regulation) Act 1986 continues to be the principal enactment on the issue of prohibition and regulation of employment of children there are a number of other labour laws that are not so much concerned with withdrawing children from work as with merely specifying the minimum age of entry to employment in certain factories, mines, plantations, etc. They are: namely Factories Act 1948, Plantation Labour Act 1951, Merchant Shipping Act 1951, Mines Act 1952, Motor Transport Workers Act 1961, Apprentices Act 1961, Beedi and Cigar Workers (Conditions of Employment) Act 1966, The Minimum Wages Act 1948, Contract Labour Act 1970, Bonded Labour System (Abolition) Act 1976, Juvenile Justice (Care and Protection of Children) Act 2000. In spite of Constitutional provisions and an updated Child Labour Protection Act 1986, India cannot avoid the shame of being home to 30 per cent of the world's child workforce. The extended ban on the employment of children below the age of fourteen years as domestic help in *dhabas*, restaurants, hotels and the hospitality sectors came into effect from 10th October, 2006 under the provisions of the Child Labour (Prohibition and Regulation) Act 1986, is one more step towards beefing up the Children's Commission Bill enacted in 2006. It also strengthens the National Plan of Action for Children 2005.

India has not ratified the ILO's two major conventions on child labour: The Minimum Age Convention 1973 (ILO Convention No. 138) and the Worst Forms of Child Labour Convention 1999 (ILO Convention No. 182). The latter prohibits the employment of children altogether. The Child Labour (Prohibition and Regulation) Act 1986 prohibits the employment of children only in certain occupation and workshops carrying out certain processes. Although the abolition of Child Labour Bill 2006 is pending in Parliament in order to give effect to the content of the Worst Forms of Child Labour Convention, from time to time the number of such occupations and processes have been added to, the last of such amendments being in 2006. Several statues expressly prohibit the employment of children below the age of 14 years such as the Apprentice Act 1961, the Factories Act 1948 and the Mines Act 1952. Despite these statutory provisions India continues to host the largest number of child labourers in the world today.

The problem of child labour is not recognised only in India but rather it was all over the world. The League of Nations in 1924 adopted *Geneva Declaration* on the Rights of Child stating that measures should be taken against social evil of slavery, child labour and traffic and prostitution of minors. In 1959 the United Nations unanimously adopted resolution on the rights of the child and reaffirmed its faith in Fundamental Human Rights and in the dignity and worth of the human. The year 1979 was declared as *International Year of the Children* and ten years later in 1989 the General Assembly of UN adopted *Convention on the Rights of the Child*. As observed by the International Labour Organization the problem of Child Labour is deeply rooted with our economic and social conditions. Population growth, industrialisation, increasing urbanisation and present scenario of globalisation have aggravated the problem of child labour in India.

Recognising the fact that child labour cannot be summarily and easily uprooted in the near future, efforts were made at Government level to minimise its scale. With this end in mind, a comprehensive law, Child Labour (Prohibition and Regulation) Act, 1986, was promulgated. This Act is concerned only with "the engagement of children in employment" and accordingly lists specific occupations (Part A) and processes (Part B) in which the employment of children is banned or is to be regulated. The occupations specified in the field include work in the railways, ports and the sale of fireworks, and the processes specified include *bidi* making, carpet weaving, and the manufacture of soaps, matches and cement. On August 1, 2006, the Ministry of Labour added the following occupations to the list of hazardous occupation: domestic servants, workers in *dhabas*, restaurants, hotels, motels, teashops, resorts, spas or other recreational centres. Violation of the ban invites imprisonment up to two years and/or fine of ₹ 10,000 to ₹ 20,000. It prohibits employment of children in certain hazardous occupations and processes and regulated their employment in some other areas. The law of 1986 sought to give a more humane face to child labour instead of issuing a blanket ban and thus inviting perpetrators to take the practice to even more covert and more dangerous contours. Its main stipulations were:

- Ban on employment of children in hazardous industries such as asbestos, tanneries, fireworks, matches, glassware;
- Every employer has to maintain a register of the children he employs, their nature of work, age, address and the like;
- Government inspectors must visit such employers periodically and inspect work conditions;
- A child should not be made to work after 7 p.m. and before 8 a.m.;
- A child should not be allowed more than 3 hours of work on the trot. He must also be given a break of one hour between two shifts of 3 hours each; and

Some basic educational facilities must be provided during after work hours by the employer.

But the ban on employment of children in hazardous occupations, or for that matter most of the provisions of the Act have still not been adequately enforced. In spite of the notification on October 10 by the Union Labour Ministry with enhanced provisions against employment of children has had little effect in the region of Varanasi and Mirzapur.

The Hon'ble Apex Court in *Bandhua Mukti Morcha* case (AIR 1992 SC) has declared that the abuse of tender age of child is bad and illegal, and observed that right to live with human dignity enshrined in Article 21 of the Constitution of India drives its life and breath from the Directive Principles of State Policy and particularly Clauses (e) and (f) of the Article 39, Article 41 and Article 42 and at least, therefore, it must include protection of health and strength of workers, men and women and of the tender age of children against abuse, opportunities and facilities for children to develop in a healthy manner and in conditions of freedom and dignity, educational facilities, just and humane conditions of work. In *Unnikrishnan, J.P.* vs. *State of Andhra Pradesh*, AIR 1993 SC 2178, and now in Article 21-A education upto the age of 14 years has been declared to be a Fundamental Right.

Conventions on the Rights of the Child, 1989

The Convention on the Rights of the Child is the first legally binding international instrument to incorporate the full range of human rights — civil, cultural, economic, political and social rights. In 1989, world leaders decided that children needed a special convention just for them because people under 18 years old often need special care and protection that adults do not. The leaders also wanted to make sure that the world recognised that children have human rights too.

The Convention sets out these rights in 54 articles and two Optional Protocols. It spells out the basic human rights that children everywhere have the right to survival, to develop to the fullest, to protection from harmful influences, abuse and exploitation, and to participate fully in family, cultural and social life. The four core principles of the Convention are non-discrimination, devotion to the best interests of the child, the right to life, survival and development, and respect for the views of the child. Every right spelled out in the Convention is inherent to the human dignity and harmonious development of every child. The Convention protects children's rights by setting standards in health care, education, and legal, civil and social services.

World Declaration on the Survival, Protection and Development of Children, 1990

It made a promise to protect the child and to end child labour. This declaration articulates various goals which pertain directly or indirectly to the protection of child in armed conflict. It also aims towards the enhancement of the health and nutrition of the child. Further attention, care and support should be accorded to disabled children, as well as to other children in very difficult circumstances. Strengthening the role of women in general and ensuring their equal rights will be to the advantage of the world's children. Girls must be given equal treatment and opportunities from the very beginning.

The declaration was followed by the adoption of a Plan of Action for the proper implementation of measures envisaged in it.

Suggestion

The development of India as a nation is being hampered by the practice of child labour and the main cause of child labour is poverty. Poverty plays a role in the ineffectiveness of the educational system. The one and only medicine to this is the eradication of poverty. The Governmental scheme should not only focus on the supplying of foods at cheap rates but to ameliorate their condition so that they can earn their livelihood. Some other suggestions are as follows:

- The state of education in India needs to be improved.
- An independent monitoring agency to oversee the enforcement of governmental policies, legislative provisions, etc., are required to be established.
- The corporate world should come forward to adopt villages and backward areas and provide job opportunities to the parents of the children.
- Awareness camp should be arranged in the rural areas as well as in urban areas with a view to impart knowledge among children regarding their rights.
- Suitable amendments should be made in laws which are for the child.

Conclusion

A child is a human being entitled to the same dignity, equality and respect due to any other human being, and equally to the same rights of survival and protection. Issues associated with child labour or elimination of it should, therefore, be viewed as a development issue or human right issue. Education is an important factor which can overcome the low incidence of child labour. The Government is not at all sensitive to the issue of children in respect of education. The Education Bill, which was mandated by Article 21A of the Constitution which lays down that the State shall provide free and compulsory education to all children in the six to fourteen years age groups, has not seen the light of the day. If the Government is serious about eradicating child labour, it should recognise that all children have a right to education and leisure and other means to develop their physical and mental capabilities during childhood. Total prohibition of child labour and the provision of free, compulsory and universally primary education should invariably go hand in hand.

Law alone is not an end to eliminate child labour or bonded labour alone unless there is a social transformation. It is basic awareness through all forms of media available that should ensure that people employing child labour start feeling ashamed rather enjoying the fruits of exploitation. To combat this social evil, we have to be more sensitive towards the children of the society, irrespective of caste and creed, region and religion which may be possible only with combined effort of the Government and society. The only solution is to ensure the provision of free and compulsory education to all, through motivation, and eliminating the poverty from society.

REFERENCES

Chowdhury, D.P., 1997. "Child Labour in India in the Asian Perspective", *Social Change*, 27, September-December.

Chowdhury, Renuka, 2006. "India's Response to Early Child Development", *Yojana*, November.

Ghosh, Jayati, 2006. "Stolen Childhood", *Frontline*, 17 November.

Gupta, Meena, 1994. "Special Problems of Enforcement of Child Labour Laws and Regulations", *Award Digest, Journal of Labour Legislation*, Vol. XX, Nos. 7-12.

Kannabiran, K.G., 1998. *Child Labour — The Legal Challenge*, Background Paper of a Workshop on Child Labour held by the A.P. State Judicial Academy, 4 April.

Mishra, Lakshmidhar, 2000. *Child Labour in India*, Oxford University Press, New Delhi.

Shrivastava, M.P., 2006. *Child Labour Laws in India*, Law Publishing House, Allahabad.

The Hindu, 2006. "Don't Hire but Educate Children", October 10, New Delhi.

The Times of India, 2006. "Government Mulls Rehabilitation Plan for Child Labourers", October 10, Kolkata.

3

RIGHTS OF CHILDREN AND THE EXISTING LAWS

Every child has the right to be protected from economic exploitation and from performing any work that is likely to be hazardous or to interfere with the child's health or physical, mental, spiritual, moral and social development.

Article 32, U.N. Convention on the Rights of the Child

Introduction

Though children constitute the weaker sections of the society yet they are the assets and future of the nation. They shape the world's future and it is quite natural that their welfare and rights are given special attention. It was only during the twentieth century that the concept of child's right emerged. The child of today is a man of tomorrow. The skill, ideas and energy of the child are vital for full attainment of the goal of equality, development and peace. For the child to develop his/her full potential needs to be nurtured in an enabling environment, where spiritual, intellectual and material needs for survival, protection and development are made and equal rights are safeguarded.

It is estimated that there are more than 250 Central and State legislations referring to children. Despite this plethora of laws their conditions is far from satisfactory. Child labour is rampant, primary education has not covered vast number of children and there is no comprehensive law of adoption. Even the existing laws are not implemented properly. Since, children themselves cannot organise and demand their rights, their destiny is entirely in the hands of conscientious adults. It is for them to be aware of the laws protecting childhood and work to enforce them. Glances at the important legislations are discussed below:

CONSTITUTION OF INDIA

Several articles of the *Constitution of India* provide protection to the children. The fundamental rights chapter deals with some of the main provisions to protect child rights. Article 24 says that no child below the age of fourteen years shall be employed to work in any factory or mines or engaged in any other hazardous employment. This principle is adopted in all other laws passed in the country. Article 23 prohibits traffic in human being and beggar (forced work or extracting work without giving the minimum prescribed wages) and declares them to be offences punishable in accordance with law. Article 15 prohibits discrimination of citizens on the ground only of religion, race, caste, sex, and place of birth or any of them. But sub-clause 3 adds: "Nothing in this article shall prevent the state from making any special provision for women and children." Therefore, laws can be made giving special protection to children. These are all fundamental rights, and if there is any violation, a writ petition may be moved in a High Court or the Supreme Court.

The Constitution has several other provisions relating to children. They are found in the chapter on Directive Principles of State Policy which cannot be enforced in courts of law. They are, however, the guiding principles for the Government. Article 39 asks the state to secure to the citizens adequate means of livelihood and fair distribution for material resources. Sub-clauses (e) and (f) are relevant to children, as it bars all forms of exploitation prejudicial to any aspects of the children's welfare. Article 39(e) asks the State to see that "the health and strength of workers, men and women and the tender age of children are not abused and that citizen are not forced by economic necessity to enter avocations unsuited to their age or strength. Article 39(f) says that children should be given "opportunity and facility to develop in a healthy manner and in condition of freedom and dignity and that youth are protected against exploitation and against moral and material abandonment". Article 45 says "the State shall endeavour to provide, within a period of ten year from the commencement of the Constitution, for free and compulsory education for all children until they complete the age of 14 years."

This free and compulsory education was for all children. But this privilege was available until they complete the age of fourteen years. The State was required to fulfil this obligation within a period of ten years from the commencement of the Constitution, i.e. by the year 1960. Article 21A was inserted in the Fundamental Right chapter which guarantees fundamental right to all children of the age six to fourteen of free and compulsory primary education subject to in such manner as the State, may by law, determine. The Constitution (Eighty Sixth Amendment) Act 2002 further introduced a new fundamental duty of the parent or guardian to provide opportunities for education to his child or ward between the ages of six to fourteen years. It is interesting to note that even it is a part of fundamental duty, Article 51A (K) does not use the world 'shall' to make it a mandatory duty.

Some of the legislations which follow these constitutional principles are —

The Factory Act 1948 prohibits employment of a child below 14 years in any factory. Restrictions are imposed on adolescents, between 14 and 18 years, to safeguard their health. For instance, a certificate of fitness from a Surgeon is required if they are to be employed. There should also be periodical medical examinations. There are restrictions on working hours for children. Those between 14 and 17 years shall not be asked to do night shift. Children between 14 and 15 years shall not be employed for more than 4½ hours on any day. They shall not be made to work near a dangerous machine unless they are fully instructed of the dangers and the precautions to be taken. There must be adequate training and supervision in such cases. Children are not allowed to do certain work in the factories. Employers who violate these rules are liable to be punished with imprisonment and fine. A factory which employs more than 50 women should also provide for a crèche.

The Mines Act is even stricter in regard to children. No one below 16 years can be present in any part of the mine. A 'child' is defined as one below 15 years of age. Those between 16 and 18 years can work in a mine if they are certified medically fit. Medical examination should be conducted every 12 months.

The Employment of Children Act 1938 is meant to prevent employment of children in hazardous work listed in a schedule, like transport. While children below 15 years are totally barred from the listed jobs, those between 15 and 17 may be employed subject to certain conditions. No one below 14 years can be employed in workshops engaged in *beedi* making, carpet weaving, cement manufacture, cloth printing, dyeing and weaving, fireworks and the like. The State Governments may add to the list of prohibited employment. Violation of these rules will entail punishment of jail and fine to the employer.

The Motor Transport Workers Act 1951 bans employment of children below 15 years. Adolescents between 15 and 18 years may be employed with a medical certificate. *The Plantation Labour Act 1951* prohibits employment of children below 12 years. Those who are between 12 and 18 years require medical certificate. Children below 14 years should not be asked to do night shift. Creches should be provided for children of women workers. *The Merchant Shipping Act 1958* bars employment of children below 15 years with certain exceptions, like when all members of the family are employed. *Beedi and Cigar Workers (Conditions of Employment) Act 1966* covers employees who work in such establishments. *The Children (Pledging of Labour) Act 1933* prohibits agreements to labour of children below 15 years. Such agreements are also void under the Contract Act as opposed to public interest. Parents who pledge their children may be fined.

The Apprentice Act 1961 regulates the training of apprentices in industry. Children below 14 years cannot be given training. Only those between 14 and 18 years are eligible. The Shops and Establishments Acts have been passed by the State governments to regulate the conditions of appointment and work in shops, restaurants and other places. Child labour is banned there.

The State Governments have passed a number of legislations for the welfare of children, keeping in view the Directive Principles of the Constitution. *State Education Acts, Anti-Smoking Acts* and the *Prevention of Beggary and Vagrancy Acts* are some of them. Children Acts of different states look after their welfare under various situations.

Several criminal laws give special protection to children. *The Criminal Procedure Code* makes it compulsory for their parents to maintain them. *The Immoral Traffic (Prevention) Act 1956* which was drastically amended in 1986, tries to curb trafficking in young persons, both boys and girls. *The Child Marriage Restraint Act 1929* prohibits the social evil. The most comprehensive law to protect children is *the Juvenile Justice Act 2000* which has updated the Children Act and incorporates modern principles of child welfare. This Act has the provision to enable the child's right to the nurturing family and environment under Section 42. *The Probation of Offenders Act* places curb on the imprisonment of young offenders and provides for their conditional release with admonition.

There are certain laws which prevent publication of obscene material and their distribution. Sections 292 and 293 of the *Indian Penal Code* deal with this problem. There is also a separate law on this, called the *Young Persons Harmful Publications Act 1956. The Customs Act, 1962* prevents import of such material into the country. *The Press and Registration of Books Act 1867* prohibits distribution of obscene information.

The Guardians and Wards Act 1890 deals with guardianship. The Hindus have two separate personal laws on this subject — The *Hindu Adoption and Minority Act 1956* and the *Hindu Minority and Guardianship Act 1956*. There is no adoption law for non-Hindus and even in the case of Hindus, it touches upon the aspect only to a limited extent. *The Evidence Act 1908* deals with legitimacy and the value of evidence given by children. Some other legislations which may be mentioned are *The Majority Act 1875, The Oaths Act 1969* and *The Vaccination Act 1880.*

The Indian judiciary have played important role in protecting the rights of the child. Some of the important judgments of the Supreme Court and High Courts regarding children are discussed below. Despite of various laws child labour is rampant in various parts of country. In the case of *M.C. Mehta* vs. *Union of India*, [AIR1997 SC 699] the judiciary has bitterly exposed the failure and has responded the issue, by issuing directions that children should not be employed in hazardous jobs in factories for manufacturing match boxes and fire works manufacturing units of Sivakasi, a town in Tamil Nadu. This judgement was closely followed by *Bandhua Mukti Morcha* vs. *Union of India*, [AIR 1997, SC 285] in which the Court reiterated the order in the *M.C. Mehta case. The Bandhua Mukti Morcha case* dealt specifically with the children in the carpet weaving industry in U.P.

In the public interest case of *Sanjay Suri* vs. *Delhi Administration* [AIR 1986 SC 414] two journalists brought out the ill-treatment given to children in prisons. The Court orders transfer of some guilty officers and lay down certain rules to protect children in jail. In *Sheela Barse* vs. *Union of India* [AIR 1986 SC 1773], the Supreme Court passes several orders about children lodged in jails and their slow trial. Again in case of *Vishaal Jeet* vs. *Union of India* [AIR 1990 SC 1414], Supreme Court passed several orders to end sexual exploitation of children. The Supreme Court orders in *People's Union for Civil Liberties* vs. *Union of India* [(1998) 8 SCC 485], tells the story of five children procured for labour. One was beaten to death and four were missing. The Court asked the State governments concerned to pay damages. The need for a law on child sexual abuse was brought to the attention of the Supreme Court in the case of *Sakshi* vs. *Union of India and Others* [AIR 1999 6 SCC 591]. The expression 'sexual intercourse' as contained in Section 375 of the IPC should include all forms of penetration as the restrictive interpretative of penetration as existing in Section 375 defeated the very purpose and intent of the provision for punishment for rape under Section 376.

The case of *Amrit Das* vs. *State of Bihar* [2000 SC 2264], raised the issue whether a person is a juvenile under the Juvenile Justice Act 1986 or not may create a problem for the Court as there is some ambiguity in the definition of the word. The Court concluded that the crucial date for determining the question whether a person is a juvenile is the date when he is brought before the competent authority, and not the date when the offence was committed.

In *Sheela Barse* vs. *Children Aid Society* [AIR 1987 SC 656], a petition was moved for the plight of children in Observation Homes the court issued several directions with regard to trial of cases against juveniles and establishment of special courts presided over by special cadre Magistrates trained suitably for dealing with cases against children. Guidelines have been laid down in *Sakshi* vs. *Union of India* [AIR 2004 SC 3566] with regards to holding trial in cases of child rape or abuse such as screen to be placed between victim and accused, sufficient breaks to be given to child testimony, etc. District Judges and Magistrates must give their special attention that these directives are strictly followed both in letter and spirit.

In *R.D. Upadhyay* vs. *State of Andhra Pradesh* (AIR 2006 SC 1946], the court issued directions for the development of children with their mothers who are in jail either as under-trial prisoners or convicts. While observing that the best interest of the child is the primary consideration of the Constitution, it was held that such children shall not be treated as an under-trial or convict while in jail with his or mother. Further, they are entitled to food, shelter, medical care, clothing, education and recreational facilities as a matter of right. In *Childline India Foundation* vs. *Alan John Waters* [AIR 2011 SC (Cri) 879] : (2011) 3 AIR Bom R 164, complaints of physical and sexual abuse of children kept in shelter homes in Mumbai were before the Supreme Court. Convicting the accused who deserve no leniency the Court observed as follows: "Children are the greatest gift to humanity. The sexual abuse of children is one of the most heinous crimes. It is an appalling violation of their trust, an ugly breach of our commitment to protect the innocent. There are special safeguards in the Constitution that apply specifically to children. The Constitution has envisaged a happy and healthy childhood for children which is free from abuse and exploitation".

The Protection of Children from Sexual Offences Act 2012

The Protection of Children from Sexual Offences Act 2012, has been passed by the Lok Sabha today, 22nd May, 2012. The Bill was earlier passed by the Rajya Sabha on 10th May, 2012.The Protection of Children from Sexual Offences Act 2012 has been drafted to strengthen the legal provisions for the protection of children from sexual abuse and exploitation. For the first time, a special law has been passed to address the issue of sexual offences against children. Sexual offences are currently covered under different sections of IPC. The IPC does not provide for all types of sexual offences against children and, more importantly, does not distinguish between adult and child victims. The Protection of Children from Sexual Offences Act, 2012 defines a child as any person below the age of 18 years and provides protection to all children under the age of 18 years from the offences of sexual assault, sexual harassment and pornography. These offences have been clearly defined for the first time in law. The Act provides for stringent punishments, which have been graded as per the gravity of the offence. The punishments range from simple to rigorous imprisonment of varying periods. There is also provision for fine, which is to be decided by the Court. An offence is treated as "aggravated" when committed by a person in a position of trust or authority of child such as a member of security forces, police officer, public servant, etc.

Punishments for Offences covered in the Act are:

- **Penetrative Sexual Assault (Section 3)** — Not less than seven years which may extend to imprisonment for life, and fine (Section 4).
- **Aggravated Penetrative Sexual Assault (Section 5)** — Not less than ten years which may extend to imprisonment for life, and fine (Section 6).
- **Sexual Assault (Section 7)** — Not less than three years which may extend to five years, and fine (Section 8).
- **Aggravated Sexual Assault (Section 9)** — Not less than five years which may extend to seven years, and fine (Section 10).
- **Sexual Harassment of the Child (Section 11)** — Three years and fine (Section 12).
- **Use of Child for Pornographic Purposes (Section 13)** — Five years and fine and in the event of subsequent conviction, seven years and fine [Section 14(1)].

The Act provides for the establishment of **Special Courts** for trial of offences under the Act, keeping the best interest of the child as of paramount importance at every stage of the judicial process. The Act incorporates **child friendly procedures** for reporting, recording of evidence, investigation and trial of offences. These include:

- Recording the statement of the child at the residence of the child or at the place of his choice, preferably by a woman police officer not below the rank of Sub-Inspector.
- No child to be detained in the police station in the night for any reason.
- Police officer not be in uniform while recording the statement of the child.
- The statement of the child to be recorded as spoken by the child.
- Assistance of an interpreter or translator or an expert as per the need of the child.
- Assistance of special educator or any person familiar with the manner of communication of the child in case child is disabled.
- Medical examination of the child to be conducted in the presence of the parent of the child or any other person in whom the child has trust or confidence.
- In case the victim is a girl child, the medical examination shall be conducted by a woman doctor.
- Frequent breaks for the child during trial.
- Child not to be called repeatedly to testify.
- No aggressive questioning or character assassination of the child.
- In-camera trial of cases.

The Act recognises that the intent to commit an offence, even when unsuccessful for whatever reason, needs to be penalised. The **attempt to commit an offence** under the Act has been made liable for punishment for up to half the punishment prescribed for the commission of the offence. The Act also provides for punishment for **abatement of the offence**, which is the same as for the commission of the offence. This would cover trafficking of children for sexual purposes. For the more heinous offences of Penetrative Sexual Assault, Aggravated Penetrative Sexual Assault, Sexual Assault and Aggravated Sexual Assault, the **burden of proof** is shifted on the accused. This provision has been made keeping in view the greater vulnerability and innocence of children. At the same time, to prevent misuse of the law, punishment has been provided for making false complaint or proving false information with malicious intent. Such punishment has been kept relatively light (six months) to encourage reporting. If false complaint is made against a child, punishment is higher (one year).The media has been barred from disclosing the identity of the child without the permission of the Special

Court. The punishment for breaching this provision by media may be from six months to one year. For speedy trial, the Act provides for the evidence of the child to be recorded within a period of 30 days. Also, the Special Court is to complete the trial within a period of one year, as far as possible.

To provide **relief and rehabilitation of the child**, as soon as the complaint is made to the Special Juvenile Police Unit (SJPU) or local police, these will make immediate arrangements to give the child, care and protection such as admitting the child into shelter home or to the nearest hospital within twenty-four hours of the report. The SJPU or the local police are also required to report the matter to the Child Welfare Committee within 24 hours of recording the complaint, for long-term rehabilitation of the child. The Act casts a duty on the Central and State Governments to spread awareness through media including the television, radio and the print media at regular intervals to make the general public, children as well as their parents and guardians aware of the provisions of this Act. The National Commission for the Protection of Child Rights (NCPCRs) and State Commissions for the Protection of Child Rights (SCPCRs) have been made the designated authority to monitor the implementation of the Act.

Conclusion

Though several laws have been passed, the number of cases under them is pitiably low. Several child welfare laws have never come to the High Courts or the Supreme Court for serious examination. This does not prove that there were no violations of these laws; rather they are not enforced to a great extent. Social evils do not disappear by merely passing the laws against them. There should be political will to implement them. The gap between legislation for children and their actual condition of life is vast. Since, children form more than one-third of the population, the future of the nation depends upon how we meet the challenge of narrowing this gap. Children need to be informed about their rights under the laws and in the legal system. This can be achieved only by propagation of awareness among the children. The District Legal Aid Committees must ensure that legal aid and advice reaches to children who seek legal representation.

4

AN EVALUATION OF MID-DAY MEAL SCHEME IN BIHAR

Introduction

The Mid-day meal programme is the popular name for schools in India. It involves provision of lunch free of cost to school children on school working days. The key objectives of the programme are: protecting children from classroom hunger, increasing school enrollment and attendance, improved socialisation among children belonging to all castes, addressing malnutrition, and social empowerment through provision of employment to women. The scheme has a long history, especially in the State of Tamil Nadu. The scheme was introduced state-wide by the then Chief Minister K. Kamaraj in the 1960s and later expanded by the M.G. Ramachandran Government in 1982.

Historical Perspective

Mid-day meals, as a public welfare concept in India, dated back to 1925 when Madras Municipal Corporation launched this programme for the underprivileged children in its area. One of the pioneers, Madras Municipal Corporation started providing cooked meals to children in Corporation schools in the Madras city; the programme was later introduced on a large scale in 1960s. Tamil Nadu's mid-day meal programme is among the best known in the country. The programme was introduced at a national level by the Government of India in the late 50s and early 60s and later in the 80s as a Centrally sponsored programme.

Besides Madras, several other States of India also have the mid-day meal programme prior to the Government of India's initiative. In 1928, Keshav Academy of Kolkata introduced compulsory mid-day Tiffin for school boys on payment basis at the rate of four annas per child per month. A school lunch programme was started in some parts of Kerala in 1941, followed by Bombay implementing a free mid-day meal scheme in 1942 who distributed skimmed milk powder to children aged between 6-13 years. Another project was launched in Bangalore city in 1946 where the scheme provided cooked rice with curds to the children. In 1953, Uttar Pradesh Government introduced a scheme, on voluntary basis, to provide meal consisting of boiled or roasted or sprouted grams, ground-nut, puffed rice, boiled potatoes or seasonal fruits. Several States introduced such scheme during 1950s, with the aid of international agencies like the United Nations Children's Fund (UNICEF) and World Health Organization (WHO). An expanded nutrition programme was launched jointly by the Government of India, WHO and UNICEF in 1958-59, which subsequently developed into the Applied Nutrition Programme (ANP). Under this, demonstration feeding programme for the school children wherein nutritious food was cooked by the women groups and fed to the children under the nutrition education component.

National Mid-day Programme

By the mid-1980s three States, *viz.* Gujarat, Kerala and Tamil Nadu and the Union Territory of Pondicherry had universalised a cooked Mid-Day Meal Programme with their own resources for children studying at the primary stage. By 1990-91 the number of States implementing the mid-day meal programme with their own resources universalised on a large scale had increased to twelve states.

1. With a view to enhancing enrollment, retention and attendance and simultaneously improving nutritional levels among children, the National Programme of Nutritional Support to Primary Education (NP-NSPE) was launched as a Centrally Sponsored Scheme on 15th August, 1995, initially in 2408 blocks in the country (GoI, 1995). By the year 1997-98 the NP-NSPE was introduced in all blocks of the country. It was further extended in 2002 to cover not only children in classes I-V of Government, Government aided and local body schools, but also children studying in EGS and AIE centres. Central Assistance under the scheme consisted of free supply of foodgrains at the rate of 100 grams per child per school day, and subsidy for transportation of foodgrains up to a maximum of ₹ 50 per quintal.
2. In September 2004 the scheme was revised to provide cooked mid-day meal with 300 calories and 8-12 grams of protein to all

children studying in classes I-V in Government and aided schools and EGS/AIE centres. In addition to free supply of food grains, the revised scheme provided Central Assistance for (a) Cooking cost at the rate of ₹ 1 per child per school day, (b) Transport subsidy was raised from the earlier maximum of ₹ 50 per quintal to ₹ 100 per quintal for special category states, and ₹ 75 per quintal for other states, (c) Management, monitoring and evaluation costs at the rate of 2 per cent of the cost of foodgrains, transport subsidy and cooking assistance, (d) Provision of mid-day meal during summer vacation in drought affected areas.

3. In July 2006 the scheme was further revised to provide assistance for cooking cost at the rate of (a) ₹ 1.80 per child/school day for States in the North-Eastern Region, provided the NER States contribute ₹ 0.20 per child/school day, and (b) ₹ 1.50 per child/school day for other States and UTs, provided that these States and UTs contribute ₹ 0.50 per child/school day.
4. In October 2007, the scheme has been further revised to cover children in upper primary (classes VI to VIII) initially in 3479 Educationally, Backward Blocks (EBBs). Around 1.7 crore upper primary children were included by this expansion of the scheme. From 2008-09, i.e. with effect from 1st April, 2008, the programme covers all children studying in Government, Local Body and Government-aided primary and upper primary schools and the EGS/AIE centres including Madarsa and Maqtabs supported under SSA of all areas across the country. The calorific value of a mid-day meal at upper primary stage has been fixed at a minimum of 700 calories and 20 grams of protein by providing 150 grams of food grains (rice/wheat) per child/school day.
5. The objectives of the mid-day meal scheme are:

   (i) Improving the nutritional status of children in classes-VIII in Government, Local Body and Government aided schools, and EGS and AIE centres.

   (ii) Encouraging poor children, belonging to disadvantaged section, to attend school more regularly and help them concentrate on classroom activities.

   (iii) Providing nutritional support to children of primary stage in drought-affected areas during summer vacation.

6. ***Rational for Mid-day Meal:***

   - *Promoting School Participation* — Mid-day meal have big

effect on school participation, not just in terms of getting more children enrolled in the registers but also in terms of regular attendance in classes.

- *Preventing Classroom Hunger* — Many children reach school on an empty stomach. Even children who have a meal before they leave for school get hungry by the afternoon and are not able to concentrate on study.
- *Facilitating the Healthy Growth of Children* — Mid-day meal can also act as a regular source of 'supplementary nutrition' for children and facilitate their healthy growth.
- *Fostering Social Equality* — Mid-day meal can help spread egalitarian value, as children from various social backgrounds learn to sit together and share a common meal. In particular, mid-day meal can help to break the barriers of caste and class among children.
- *Intrinsic Educational Value* — A well organised mid-day meal can be used as an opportunity to impart various habits to children and to educate them about the importance of clean water, good hygiene and other related matters.
- *Psychological Benefits* — Psychological deprivation leads to low self-esteem, consequently insecurity, anxiety and stress. Mid-day meal can help to remove psychological abnormality.

7. ***Nutritional Content*** — To achieve the objective of mid-day meal with nutritional content is provided to all eligible children.

Component	*Primary*	*Upper Primary*
Calories	450	700
Protein	12 gms	20 gms
Micro-nutrients	Adequate quantities of micro-nutrients like Iron, Folic Acid and Vitamins	

Although the programme in Tamil Nadu was initially termed as an act of "Populism", the success of the scheme made the project highly popular. The success was so spectacular that in 1995, the then Indian Prime Minister P.V. Narasimha Rao hailed the success of the project and suggested that the scheme be implemented all over the country, and thus began the "National Programme for Nutrition Support to Primary Education". According to the programme the Government of India will provide grains free of cost and the States will provide the costs of other ingredients, salaries and infrastructure. Since, most State Governments were unwilling to commit budgetary resources they just passed on the grains from Government of India to the parents. This system was called provision of 'dry rations'.

The Supreme Court Direction

In April 2001 People's Union for Civil Liberties (Rajasthan) initiated the now famous right to food litigation. This public interest litigation has covered a large range of issues relating to right to food, but the best known intervention by the Court is on mid-day meals. In one of its many direction in the litigation the Supreme Court directed the Government to fully implement its scheme of providing cooked meals to all children in primary schools. The Apex Court gave a famous direction that made it mandatory for the State Governments to provide cooked meals instead of 'dry rations'. This landmark direction converted the Mid-day Meal Scheme into a legal entitlement, the violation of which can be taken up in the Court of Law. The direction and further follow-up by the Supreme Court has been a major instrument in universalising the scheme. With the sustained pressure from the Court, media and in particular from the Right to Food Campaign more and more states started providing cooked meals.

In May 2004, a new coalition Government was formed in the Centre, which promised universal provision of cooked meals fully funded by the Centre. This promise in its Common Minimum Programme was followed by enhanced financial support to the States for cooking and building sufficient infrastructure. Given this additional support the scheme has expanded its reach to cover most children in primary schools in India.

Bihar MDM Objective

The main objective of MDM Programme in Bihar is to boost universalisation of Primary Education. Mid-Day Meal Programme was expected to attract more children to come to school and in this way it will increase enrollment, attendance, retention and bring down drop-out rate. Mid-Day Meal Programme with enhanced calorific energy content and increased quantity of proteins in food, is also expected to improve the nutritional status of children. Mid-Day Meal Programme will surely encourage poor children belonging to disadvantaged sections of the society to attend school more regularly. The rationale of the Mid-Day Meal Programme is that if it is successfully implemented, it would help in increasing the enrollment of children in school and minimising the number of out of school children and drop-out rate. Parents of poor children will find less difficulty in sending their children to schools if meal is served to them.

Assessment of the Programme

On the whole, Mid-Day Meal Programme which has been implemented in the State has been able to a great extent to attract more children to schools. Drop-out rate has come down considerably. Mid-Day Meal Programme also helps the poor families by lessening their hesitation to send their children to school where they do not have to worry about providing food to the children during school hours.

National Programme of Nutritional Support to Primary Education, popularly known as the Mid-Day Meal Scheme (MDM) was started in 1995 in an attempt to enhance enrollment, retention and attendance while simultaneously improving nutritional levels among children in school. It currently covers nearly 12 crore children.

In October 2007, the scheme was revised to cover children in the upper primary section as well, i.e. classes VI to VII. The Scheme estimates a cooked mid-day meal with a minimum of 300 calories and 8-12 grams of protein to all children studying in classes I-V. Upper Primary meals consist of 700 calories and 20 grams of protein by providing 150 grams of foodgrains (rice/wheat) per child/school day. The Central Government supplies State and Union Territory Governments with free foodgrains (wheat/rice) at 100 grams per child per school day from the nearest Food Corporation of India (FCI) godown and compensation of the cost of transporting the foodgrains from the nearest FCI to the Primary school. The scheme provides assistance for meeting the cooking cost of ₹ 1 per child per school day.

The programme is being carried out by local authorities with assistance from village panchayats, village education committees, school management committees, NGOs, parent-teacher associations and with the help of teaching community. In rural areas the cooking is also done by women self-help groups (SHG). Free mid-day meals can achieve a great deal with regard to child education and health. They promote the participation of the child in school, reduce classroom hunger, facilitate the healthy growth of a child, promotes good eating habits like washing ones hands, finishing ones food and fosters social and gender equality as all children get the same food and must eat together. In April 2012, the

Chief Minister, Bihar launched an Interactive Voice Response System (IVRS) for the education department to monitor the implementation of mid-day meal scheme in 72,000 Government schools. The system entails a monitoring mechanism whereby every principal is connected on phone to confirm the status of mid-day meal in that school. The details gathered through IVRS are put in the public domain for scrutiny. However, like all high sounding schemes, the IVRS too has failed to ensure transparent and foolproof delivery of the scheme.

Bihar Mid-Day Meal Disaster

Mid-day meal tragedy at Government Primary School in Gandaman-Dharmsati village under Mashrakh block at Chapra in Saran district, Bihar where 23 children lost their lives after eating mid-day meal. The school, housed in a temporary shelter, mostly had student from the minority and extremely backward class communities. It was opened in 2010, but is yet to get its building. After the incident, students in other school stopped eating their mid-day meal and State Government published an advertisement saying that it is mandatory for the principal and cooks of all schools to taste mid-day meals before serving them to children and also to maintain quality of food.

A forensic report confirmed the presence of poisonous pesticide in the mid-day meal served to the student of the school in Chapra. The Forensic Science Laboratory report found Monocrotophos, an organophosphorous compound in the sample such as cooking oil taken from a container in the kitchen, leftover on the children's plates, a rice and vegetable mixture found in some cooking utensils at the school, water used for cooking and drinking. Monocrotophos is used as a pesticide for agricultural purposes. It is very toxic to human being and other animal. Circumstantial evidence, however, suggested that the cooking oil had been kept in a container used to store pesticides (*The Telegraph*, 2013:4).

The quality of mid-day meals served under the scheme has been a cause of concern for a long time. In 2010, the Planning Commission report on the scheme, which in 2013-14 has a total budgetary allocation of ₹ 13,215 crore and is implemented across 17 states, showed that most schools had inadequate infrastructure, served bad food and lacked basic hygiene (*The Hindustan Times*, 2013:8).

R. Lakshmanan, Director of the State mid-day meal, said the school in Gandaman-Dharmsati village would be merged with the nearest middle school having a better mid-day meal infrastructure (*The Hindustan Times*, 2013:1). He further said that Government had taken a policy decision not to run school from rented and dilapidated structure and equip new units with full-fledged kitchens and appealed to the school management committee, comprising mothers of students and elected representatives of panchayats, to taste the food being served and monitor quality. The Bihar Government is planning to provide printed instructions to school principals about food quality and safety besides painting norms on the schools walls for everyone to see and follow.

In the wake of the tragedy, the Bihar Government has announced its decision to close down all open air schools, where cooking was also done in the open. As many as 220 schools across the State have reportedly been closed (*The Statesman*, 2013:7).

The Human Resource Development Ministry is the nodal agency for implementing the mid-day meal programme has sought a report from the Bihar Government on 16th July, 2013 mid-day meal tragedy in Chapra in which 23 children died. "It is a very sad incident and we are deeply pained at the loss of lives of children", HRD Minister M.M. Pallam Raju told on 17th July. He said it looked like a case of food contamination and asked the States to exercise caution while implementing the mid-day meal scheme. "It is an aberration. Although it is an unfortunate incident, it is not a recurring thing." The Ministry is also putting in place a system to check the quality of mid-day meals. This includes availability of a building where cooking can be done for schools that are in the open, proper storage facility for provisions and availability of vessels, mothers of the students will also be roped in to taste the meals as well as supervise the cooking.

HRD Ministry officials said they had earlier alerted the Bihar Government about the poor quality of food being served in schools in 12 districts including Saran. Mid-Day Scheme guidelines say that cooked food should be tested by two adults before serving, while the teachers should also look into the quality of food and cleanliness of the utensils but many schools do not follow guidelines. The involvement of parents in monitoring the scheme is also minimal.

In another incident, as many as 122 children were taken ill and had to be admitted to hospitals after they consumed contaminated mid-day meals in primary schools in two different districts of Bihar on July 31st, 2013. The first case was reported from Central Bihar's Arwal district where at least 65 children fell ill after eating free mid-day meal at a primary school located at Chamandi village. After the food was eaten, around 10 children fainted while other started complaining about stomach pain and vomiting. They were rushed to local primary health centre. Doctors said the children were victims of food poisoning. In second case, at least 57 children fell ill after eating mid-day meals at an upgraded primary school, Kalhuiya, in eastern Jamui district. The children began vomiting and also suffered from stomach disorders. The food has been served by a local NGO (*The Statesman*, 2013:4).

People's Protest in Saran

Widespread protests erupted in Chapra, Saran district, on 17 July, 2013 after 23 children died from poisoning after consuming a mid-day meal in their school. Allegedly, the cook complained to the headmistress about the smell of the oil used to cook the meal, before going ahead for cooking. But the headmistress allegedly dismissed her concerns. Political parties who flayed both the Government for its delay in responding to the tragedy, and Chief Minister Nitish Kumar for his silence over the issue, called for a *banda* in Chapra. People from Gandaman village where the school is located, and people from neighbouring villages, staged violent protests in Mashrakh block. "All the victims are from the Gandaman village. A police team had gone there in the morning to help with the cremations. However, as early as 6.30 a.m. a mob started pelting stones. There was heavy brick batting. People set fire to four police vehicles. The police had to retreat in light of the protests," Superintendent of Police Sujeet Kumar said:

> Special Investigation Team (SIT) has been set-up to investigate the mid-day meal tragedy. Police finally arrested the absconding principal of Dharmnasati-Gandaman Primary School and investigation is going on. State Chief Minister Sri Nitish Kumar said that we cannot get back the lives lost, but we will work hard for the reconstruction and all-round development of the village. The village will have a new high school, a health sub-centre, potable water facility and will be linked with *pucca* road (*The Statesman*, 2013:2).

Lacuna in Bihar MDM

In June 2013, survey of 14 schools, including in Nalanda and Purnea districts of Bihar, found the following defects in the State's Mid-day meal scheme (Shrivastava, 2013:38):

- Inefficiency in fund flow to school causing poor quality of food and implementation. Only sixty per cent enrolled students received daily meals.
- Mid-day meal not served regularly.
- Inadequate staff, weak monitoring system, lack of feedback from schools to district.
- Fund tracking solutions difficult to evaluate, impossible to identify bottlenecks.
- Cook-*cum*-helper, one per school, is not paid in time. Most cooks paid after two months. In some districts, cooks paid after six months.
- Most of the schools are serving poor quality meal that comprises rice laced with pebbles, poor quality *dal* and low quality soyabean.

Government Initiatives

After the disaster in Bihar, Ministry of Human Resource Development comes out with new policy. The Mid-Day Meal Rules 2015 have been notified under the National Food Security Act 2013 which effects from 30th September, 2015. Some of the main features of the Mid-Day Meal Rules are —

1. Rule 7 provides for the role of School Management Committee (SMC) for monitoring Mid-Day Scheme. The School Management Committee mandate under Right to Free and Compulsory Education Act 2009 shall also monitor implementation of the mid-day meal scheme and shall oversee quality of meal provided to the children, cleanliness of the place of cooking and maintenance of hygiene in implementation of mid-day meal scheme. The headmaster or headmistress of the school shall be empowered to utilize any fund available in school for the purpose of continuation of Mid-Day Scheme in the school in case of temporary unavailability of foodgrains, cooking cost, etc. in the school. The utilized fund shall be reimbursed to the school account immediately after receipt of mid-day meal funds.
2. Rule 8 emphasized on the quality of food to ensure that the meal meets the nutritional standards and quality prescribed by the MDM Rules. The Food and Drug Administration Departments of the State may collect samples from randomly selected school to ensure adherence to quality.

3. Rule 9 is about food security allowance to be paid by State Government, if MDM is not provided in any school for three consecutive days or five days in a month. The State Government shall take action to fix responsibility on the person or agency in accordance with the procedure laid down.

These Statutory Rules need to be disseminated and enforced in all eligible school (GoI, 2015).

Suggestion

There should be parameter for proper execution of mid-day meal scheme which includes:

- School heads must taste the food before serving.
- Cooking with ISI certified edible oil.
- Cooked food must be stored in covered utensils.
- Kitchens, storages and utensils must be clean.
- Government should set-up inspection teams for every district. The team will visit school in batches on every working day and examine whether proper hygiene is maintained during cooking and serving.
- To increase efficiency and quality of the prepared meal service, contracted private parties may be required to follow formal food quality management system.
- The mandated mid-day meals are supposed to provide only a minimum of 700 calories out of the total requirement of about 2000 calories per day. Therefore, efficacy of the nutrition delivery could be increased by offering fortified packaged foods.

Conclusion

Thus, the Government mid-day meal scheme in schools is an essential component to meet the nutrition needs of thousands of children across the country. A society must be judged by the way we treat our children. Those who prepared to feed our children unsafe food should not be allowed anywhere near them. What happened in Bihar was criminal act. But it cannot make an excuse to stop the mid-day meal scheme. On contrary, better quality of foodgrains and ingredients, along with hygienic cooking is the only way to keep children healthy and safe in their schools. Centralised food cooking and then distributing in school for mid-day meal can be an effective measure for checking poisonous food served to child like in Bihar. Government has to take steps for monitoring the mid-day meal scheme. For this Government can engage civil society and private agencies to beef up the monitoring system. Food Inspector may be deployed to periodically check the quality of prepared meals. Union Ministry of Human Resource Development should frame new guidelines to improve effectiveness, safety, quality and hygiene of the meal served to children in the schools.

REFERENCES

Dreze, J. and A. Goyal, 2003. "Future of Mid-day Meals", *Economic and Political Weekly*, Vol. 10, No. 6.

Garg, Manish and Mandal, Kalyan, Sankar, 2013. "Mid-Day Meal for the Poor, Privatised Education for the Non-Poor", *Economic and Political Weekly*, July 27, Vol. XLVIII, No. 30.

GoI, 1995. "Guidelines of National Programme of Nutritional Support to Primary Education (Mid-Day Meal Scheme)".

GoI, 2004. "Guidelines of Revised National Programme of Nutritional Support to Primary Education [Mid-Day Meal Scheme]".

GoI, 2015. "Ministry of Human Resource Development (Department of School Education and Literacy)".

GoI, 1996. "Task Force Report on Micronutrients".

Khera, R., 2006. "Mid-Day Meal in Primary School", *Economic and Political Weekly*, Vol. 41, No. 46.

Khera, Reetika, 2013. "Mid-Day Meal: Looking Ahead", *Economic and Political Weekly*, August 10, Vol. XLVIII, No. 32.

Planning Commission, 2010. "Performance Evaluation of Cooked Mid-Day Meal", Programme Evaluation Organisation, PEO Report No. 202, Planning Commission, GoI.

SC, 2001. *People's Union for Civil Liberties* vs. *Union of India*, Judgement of the Writ Petition (Civil No. 196 of 2001), Supreme Court (SC).

Shrivastava, Amitabh, 2013. "School of Murder", *India Today*, 29 July.

Swaminathan, M., 1999. "Food and Nutrition", Vol. 2 and Appendix 1.

Shukla, Siddheshwar, 2014. "Mid-Day Meal: Nutrition on Paper, Poor Food on the Plate", *Economic and Political Weekly*, February, Vol. XLIX, No. 7.

The Hindustan Times, 2013. "It's All that is Not Fit to Eat", July 19, Kolkata, p. 8.

The Hindustan Times, 2013. "Killer Meal: Principal's Property to be Attached", July 21, Kolkata, p. 1.

The Statesman, 2013. "Centre Seeks Report on Bihar Mid-day Meal Tragedy", July 18, Kolkata, p. 1.

The Statesman, 2013. "No Excuses for Gandaman Children Deaths", July 18, Kolkata, p. 7.

The Statesman, 2013. "Mid-day Meal Tragedy: Principal Arrested", July 25, Kolkata, p. 7.

The Statesman, 2013. "122 Children Ill After Mid-day Meals", August 1, Kolkata, p. 4.

The Telegraph, 2013. "Meal Report Confirms Insecticide Presence", July 21, Kolkata, p. 4.

websites

www.mdm.nic.in

www.pib.nic.in/archieve/flagship/bkg_mdm1.pdf

5

CRITICAL APPRAISAL OF GIRL'S STALKING

Introduction

Stalking is defined as a 'willful course of conduct' involving repeated or continuing harassment of another individual that would cause a reasonable person to feel terrorised, frightened, intimidate, threatened, harassed or molested and that actually cause the victim to feel terrorised, frightened, intimidate, threatened, harassed or molested. Stalking is unwanted or obsessive attention by an individual or group towards another person. Stalking behaviours are related to harassment and intimidation and may include following the victim in person or monitoring them. Stalking is a pattern of repeated and unwanted attention, harassment, contact, or any other course of conduct directed at a specific person that would cause a reasonable person to feel fear. Stalking includes —

(i) Repeated, unwanted, intrusive, and frightening communications from the perpetrator through phone, mail, or email.

(ii) Repeatedly leaving or sending victim unwanted items, presents, or flowers.

(iii) Following or laying in wait for the victim at places such as home, school, work, or recreation place.

(iv) Making direct or indirect threats to harm the victim, the victim's children, relatives, friends, or pets.

(v) Damaging or threatening to damage the victim's property.

(vi) Harassing victim through the internet. Posting information or spreading rumours about the victim on the internet, in a public place, or by word of mouth. Obtaining personal information about the victim by accessing public records, using internet search services, hiring private investigators, going through the victim's garbage, following the victim, contacting victim's friends, family work, or neighbours, etc.

Almost all stalkers have some type of mental or emotional problem. Stalkers go across town, country, or even to different continents in order to continue their stalking. Stable people simply do not continue, often in the face of years of rejection, to pursue someone. Stalkers, no matter what or how severe their mental disorder, can usually be sorted into one of three major groupings: Simple Obsession, Love Obsession, and Other.

Simple Obsession Stalkers

These stalkers have previously been involved in an intimate relationship with their victims. Often the victim has attempted to call off the relationship but the stalker simply refuses to accept it. These stalkers suffer from personality disorders, including being emotionally immature, extremely jealous, insecure, have low self-esteem and quite often feel powerless without the relationship. While reconciliation is the goal, this stalker believes they must have a specific person back or they will not survive. The stalker of former spouses or intimate partners, are often domineering and abusive to their partners during the relationship and use this domination as a way to bolster their own low self-esteem. They control the abusers exert over their partners gives them a feeling of power they can't find elsewhere. They try to control every aspect of their partner's lives. Their worst fear is losing people over whom they have control.

When they realise this fear as the relationship finally does end, the stalker suddenly believes that his/her life is destroyed. Their total identity and feelings of self-worth are tied up in the power experienced through their domineering and abusive relationship. Without this control, they feel that they will have no self-worth and no identity. They will become nobodies and in desperation they begin stalking, trying to regain their partner and the basis of their power. It is this total dependence on their partner for identity and feelings of self worth that makes these stalkers so very dangerous. They will often go to any length and stop at nothing to get their partner back. If they can't have the people over whom they can exert dominance and total control, their lives are truly not worth living. Unfortunately, along with becoming suicidal, they also often want to kill the intimate partners who have left them.

Love Obsession Stalkers

These are individuals who become obsessed with or fixed on a person with whom they have had no intimate or close relationship. The victim may be a friend, a business acquaintance; people met only once, or even a complete stranger. Love obsession stalkers believe that a special, often mystical, relationship exists between them and their victims. Any contact with the victim becomes a positive reinforcement of this relationship and any wavering (even the slightest) of the victim from an absolute "NO" is seen as an invitation to continue the pursuit. These stalkers will often read sexual meanings into neutral responses from the victim. They are often loners with an emotional void in their lives. Any contact with the object of the infatuation, even negative, helps fill this void. Failed relationships are the rule among these individuals.

Many suffer from *erotomania*. They have the delusion that they are loved intensely by another person, usually a person of higher socio-economic status than them or an unattainable public figure. They are totally convinced that the stalking victim loves them dearly and truly, and would return their affection except for some external influence. During questioning, police find that most love obsession stalkers have fantasised a complete relationship with the person they are stalking. When they attempt to act out this fantasy in real life, they expect the victim to return the affection. When no affection is returned, the stalker often reacts with threats and intimidation. When the threats and intimidation don't accomplish what they hoped, the stalker can often become violent and even deadly.

Other Stalkers

Some stalkers harass their victim not out of love but out of hate. Occasionally, stalking becomes a method of revenge for some misdeed against the stalker, real or imagined. Stalking can also be used as a means of protest. This is the smallest group, but this type of stalking, for revenge and protest, can be especially dangerous. There have been several killings by stalkers at abortion clinics, and mass murders around the country by employees who have been fired and then returned to stalk and eventually kill those who have fired them.

Cyberstalking

Cyberstalking is the use of the internet or other electronic means to stalk or harass a girl. It may include the making of false accusation or statements of fact (as in defamation), monitoring, making threats, damage to data or equipment, the solicitation of minors for sex, or gathering information that may be used to harass. The definition of "harassment" must meet the criterion that a reasonable person, in possession of the same information, would regard it as sufficient to cause another reasonable person distress. Cyberstalking is different from spatial or offline stalking in that it occurs through the use of electronic communications technology such as the internet. However, it sometimes leads to it, or is accompanied by it. Both are criminal offences. Cyberstalking shares important characteristics with offline stalking; many stalkers — online or offline — are motivated by a desire to control their victims.

Harassment on the internet can take a variety of guises. The term online harassment and cyberstalking often used interchangeably, therefore, there is no particular definition of both the terms is available. One of the simplest definition of cyberstalking is the use of electronic communication including pages, cell phone, emails and the internet, to bully, threaten, harass and intimidate a victim. It can be divided into direct and indirect harassment. Direct harassment includes: threats, bullying, or intimidating messages sent directly to the victim *via* email which are abusive, threatening or obscene from one person to another or other internet communication mediums and the use of technological means to interfere with a victim's use of the internet — such as hacking or denial of services attacks. Indirect harassment includes spreading rumours about the victim in various internet discussion forums; subscribing the victim to unwanted online services, posting information about the victim in online dating or sex services, or sending messages to others in the victim's name and alike activities *via* internet (Saxena, 2010:259).

Electronic means has also become one of the factors for the crime of cyberstalking which is again in the form of online harassment. The distinction between harassment and cyberstalking is that cyberstalking is characterised by pursuit and fear. It becomes cyberstalking when repeated unwanted communications, whether direct or indirect takes place over a period of time *via* one or more mediums of internet or electronic communication of frequency of threat convert online harassment into cyberstalking. The communication themselves must be unwanted and the content can be threatening, sexually harassing, emotionally harassing or bullying, or general misinformation. Providing such communications create reasonable fear in the victim. As the internet becomes an ever more integral part of our personal and professional lives, stalkers can take advantage of the ease of communications as well as increased access to personal information. As well the ease of use and non-confrontational, impersonal and sometimes anonymous nature of internet communications may remove disincentive to cyberstalking. In a different way, where a potential stalker may be unwilling or unable to confront a victim in person or on the telephone, he or she may have slight hesitation sending harassing or threatening electronic communication to a victim.

Causes of Stalking

Many stalkers are loners. Because of the lack of other relationships, they become severely attached to the idea of possessing a relationship with the person who they are stalking. In many cases, the lack of ability to form relationships starts at a young age. Some stalkers are neglected by their parents, and in turn are unable to form attachments with other people later on in life. This causes them to be extremely lonely, which is a main characteristic of a stalker. This lack of personal relationships, combined with a low self-esteem creates a feeling of worthlessness. They feel like without a connection with the person they are stalking, they have no purpose in life. This is one reason for most celebrity stalking. Some of the tasks that are carried out by stalkers are quite difficult. Stalkers need way more intelligence than one would assume that they have. But although many of them have mental disorders, most stalkers are much smarter than the average person. Obtaining information about a person is not usually the easiest task, but stalkers may go as far as changing jobs in order to do so. Stalkers sometimes learn how to tap into phone conversations, hack into computers.

Stalking is not always based on positive feelings and desire to by love. Some people stalk to seek revenge or simply out of pure hatred for a person. Sometimes, stalking can occur in the workplace. A large number of murders due to stalking are carried out by people who have recently been fired from a job and who want to get revenge on the person who fired them.

The vast majority of individual who stalk do not behave in this way most of the time and in fact, their behaviour is usually restricted to specific victim in a specific context. The role of contextual factors such as relationship breakdown, unemployment, perceived failure or embarrassment and social isolation all play a central role in the commencement and perpetuation of stalking. Sexual perversion is also one of the reasons for doing stalking like behaviour.

Nature of Cyberstalking

The nature of cyberstalking had been classified into four categories including email stalking, chat stalking, bulletin board system and computer stalking. The information of each other extends cyberstalking to real life.

(a) ***Email Stalking:*** Electronic mail is an electronic postal service that allows individuals to send and receive information in seconds. This sophisticated use of telephone lines allows communication between more than one people who may or may not know each other but can speak to each other using computer. With some online services as AOL, a person's screen name is also an email address. In addition, when a person posts an item on a newsgroup, that person's email ID may be available to anyone who reads that item.

(b) ***Chat Stalking:*** A chat room is a link provided by online services and available on the internet that allows people to communicate in real time *via* computer text and modem. Cyberstalker can use chat rooms to slander and endanger their victims. In such cases the cyberstalking takes on a public rather than a private dimension. As live chat has become more popular amongst users of the internet with tools such as internet relay chat, it has also become more popular as a medium through which stalker can identify and pursue their prey. Thus, on the internet, public messages can be accessed by anyone anytime — even years after the messages were originally written. In internet relay chat, the harasser may chose to interrupt a person's chat electronically or otherwise target a chat system, making it impossible for someone to carry on a conversation with anyone else, the cyberstalker can engage in live chat harassment or abuse of the victim.

(c) ***Bulletin Board System:*** A bulletin board system is a local computer that can be called directly with a modem. Usually, they are privately operated and offer various services depending on the owner and the users. A bulletin board allows leaving messages in group forums to be read at a later time. Often a bulletin board system is not connected to a network of other computers, but increasingly bulletin board systems are offering internet access and co-cyberstalkers area using bulletin boards to harass their victims. A cyberstalker can 'dupe' another internet users into harassing or threatening a victims by posting a controversial or enticing message on the board under the name, phone numbers or email address of the victim, resulting in subsequent responses being sent to the victim.

There is possibility of using chat room discussion to obtain sufficient information about the target and gather information from other internet sites. The stalker can then use the information to locate the victim and engage in 'real-life' stalking behaviour. The threats made online have the potential to carry over into real life. The stalker's threats over the internet may perhaps become more severe because barricades may be poorer as a result of the lack of contact and the anonymity provided by the internet.

Psychological Effect

Stalking is a very dangerous situation to be involved with. The effect it has on girls can be long lasting and can also cause them to change their life completely. The fear can be caused by many things, one being that knowing you are being watched and followed can by very disturbing, another is that if the victim is receiving threatening messages or has already had a violent encounter with her victim it can cause her to fear living her normal day-to-day life. As a result victims often changed different aspect of their life, things like where they live, and where they work. Some girls can be so scared from the experience that she might go into some kind of hiding and never really be fully functional in society. Some other psychological effects are anxiety, difficult sleeping, some may turn to the use of drugs and alcohol and some victims can develop mild cases of post-traumatic stress disorder and lost control in their own life. They may also develop depression symptoms and as a result sometimes it could lead to suicide. Victims often lose time from work or never returned to work and some even relocate to regain their sense of safety.

Legal Measures

Previously, there was no penal provision to combat with the crime of stalking, which is not possible because of the recent Criminal Law Amendment Act 2013.

354D. (1) Any man who —

(i) Follows a woman and contacts, or attempts to contact such woman to foster personal interaction despite a clear indication of disinterest by such woman; or

(ii) Monitors the use by a woman of the internet, email or any other form of electronic communication, commits the offence of stalking:

Provided that such conduct shall not amount to stalking if the man who pursued it proves that —

(i) It was pursued for the purpose of preventing or detecting crime and the man accused of stalking had been entrusted with the responsibility of prevention and detection of crime by the State; or

(ii) It was pursued under any law or to comply with any condition or requirement imposed by any person under any law; or

(iii) In the particular circumstances such conduct was reasonable and justified.

The recognition of word cyberstalking cannot be said to be a new concept rather it got its place under Information Technology Act 2000. Section 29(a) of the Indian Penal Code defines Electronic Record as "The words "Electronic Record" shall have the meaning assigned to them in Clause (t) of sub-section (1) of Section 2 of the Information Technology Act 2000."

This big change is the recognition of electronic document as evidence in a court of law.

Enforcement Problems

It is appreciable that the Government framed laws for stalking, but it is very difficult to prove it. If the crime occurred on roadside then victims cannot prove stalking in court of law due to lack of evidence. Let's finally remember new laws won't help unless we demonstrate how effectively existing ones are enforced. Implementation is the key. The enforcement problems related to cyberstalking is related to international aspect of the internet. Internet is a medium that can be accessed by anyone throughout the globe with a computer and modem. So, a potential offender may not be within the jurisdiction where an offence is committed. Anonymous use of the internet, though beneficial in many instances, also promises to create challenges for law enforcement authorities.

Suggestion

- Inform law enforcement officials about the stalking and provide them evidence to support a case.

- Develop a safety plan. Inform friends, neighbours, and co-workers about the situation. Show them a photo of the stalker.
- Have easy access to a reserve set of: money, credit cards, medication, important papers, keys, and other valuables in case you need to leave quickly. Have a safe place in mind that you can go in an emergency.
- Keep the phone numbers of assistance agencies easily accessible.
- Girl should avoid walking alone in dark areas at night or in isolated areas any time of the day.
- Harassment/stalking often begin as minor annoying encounters, be attentive to early warning signs prior to the escalation of the stalking.
- Any suspicious activities should be reported to the police.
- Threats (from minor or vague to severe or specific) should be treated seriously and immediately reported to the law enforcement.

Preventive Measures of Cyberstalking

Here are a few important pointers to help you thwart cyberstalking, whether it is directed at you, your PC, or your family:

- Maintain vigilance over physical access to your computer and other Web-enabled devices like cell phones. Cyberstalkers use software and hardware devices (sometimes attached to the back of your PC without you even knowing) to monitor their victims.
- Be sure you always log out of your computer programmes when you step away from the computer and use a screensaver with a password. The same goes for passwords on cell phones. Your kids and your spouse should develop the same good habits.
- Make sure to practice good password management and security. Never share your passwords with others. And be sure to change your passwords frequently! This is very important.
- Do an online search for your name or your family members now and then to see what's available about you and your kids online. Don't be shy about searching social networks (including your friends and colleagues), and be sure to remove anything private or inappropriate.

- Delete or make private any online calendars or itineraries — even on your social network — where you list events you plan to attend. They could let a stalker know where you are planning to be and when.
- Use the privacy settings in all your online accounts to limit your online sharing with those outside your trusted circle. You can use these settings to opt out of having your profile appear when someone searches for your name. You can block people from seeing your posts and photos, too.
- If you suspect that someone is using spyware software to trace your everyday activities, and you feel as if you are in danger, only use public computers or telephones to seek help. Otherwise, your efforts to get help will be known to your cyberstalker and this may leave you in even greater danger.
- Extra training to law enforcement agencies should be given to enable them to deal with victim report of online harassment efficiently and with sensitivity.

Conclusion

Stalking is a very frightening occurrence that affects a huge amount of people each year. Although, they may come from all different backgrounds, genders, races, cultures, and even sexual orientations, these people possess certain traits which identify them are stalkers. These dangerous qualities, combined with their unfortunate reasoning can sadly lead to the psychological damage and sometimes even death of innocent people. Stalking is a prevalent and damaging form of behaviour to which all members of the society are susceptible. It is, often described as a further act of violence causing emotional and psychological abuse. Social awareness is needed to change the mentality of common people. It should be begun from family level where male and female child should be treated equally. Counselling should be done by family members, friends and by psychologist.

REFERENCES

GoI, 2013. "The Criminal Law (Amendment) Act".

Goode, M., 1995. "Stalking: The Crime of the Nineties", *Cambridge Law Journal*, p. 21.

Jain, Atul, 2005. *Cyber Crime*, Isha Books, New Delhi.

MacGraw, D., 1995. "Sexual Harassment in Cyberspace: The Problem of Unwelcome Email".

Mishra, R.C., 2002. *Cyber Crime: Impact in the New Millennium*, p. 53.

Mullen, P.E. and Pathe, M., 1997. "The Impact of Stalker on their Victim", *British Journal of Psychiatry*, pp. 12-17.

Reed, Chris, 2004. *Internet Law*, Cambridge University Press, UK.

Saxena, Nidhi, 2010. "Harassment in Virtual World (Cyberstalking) : Emerging Threat for Real World's Dignity and Rights", *Indian Human Rights Law Review*, R. Cambray & Co. Private Ltd., Vol. 1, No. 2, Kolkata.

Yatindra, Singh, 2007. *Cyber Laws*, Universal Law Publishing Co., New Delhi.

Websites

www.abuse.net
www.cyber-right.org
www.en.wikipedia.org/wiki/stalking
www.esia.net
www.stalkingvictims.com
www.wiredpatrol.org

6

CHILD PORNOGRAPHY

Introduction

Child pornography refers to the possession, trade, advertising and production of images that depict the sexual abuse of children. It may use a variety of media, including writing, magazines, photos, sculpture, drawing, animation, sound recording, video and video games, cartoon, painting. Child pornography is divided into simulated child pornography and pornography which was produced with direct involvement of the child (also known as child abuse images). Abuse of the child occurs during the sexual acts which are recorded in the production of child pornography. Ninety-four of 187 Interpol member states had laws specifically addressing child pornography, though this does not include nations that ban all pornography. Of those 94 countries, 58 criminalised possession of child pornography regardless of intent to distribute. Both distribution and possession are now criminal offenses in almost all western countries. A wide movement is working to globalise the criminalisation of child pornography, including major international organisations such as the United Nations and the European Commission.

Legal definitions of child pornography generally include sexual images involving prepubescents and pubescent or post-pubescent minors and computer-generated images that appear to involve them. Most possessors of child pornography who are arrested are found to possess images of prepubescent children; possessors of pornographic images of post-pubescent minors are less likely to be prosecuted, even though those images also fall within the statutes.

Child pornography is defined by the Optional Protocol on the Sale of Children, Child prostitution and Child pornography as any representation of a child engaged in real or simulated explicit sexual activities or of the sexual parts of a child for primarily sexual purposes. Child pornography is the evidence of the sexual abuse of a child and the production of child pornography always presupposes a crime committed towards the child. It objectifies and degrades children. Child pornography may be used by abusers as a means to manipulate a child by claiming that what is happening to the child in the picture is something that many children take part (Sood, 2010:31).

Definition of Child Pornography

- ***Indicative:*** Non-sexualised pictures collected from legitimate sources (e.g., magazine, catalogues, etc.).
- ***Nudist:*** Naked or semi-naked pictures of children in appropriate setting collected from legitimate sources.
- ***Erotica:*** Pictures taken secretly of children in which they reveal varying degree of nakedness.
- ***Posing:*** Posed pictures of children in varying degree of nakedness.
- ***Erotic Posing:*** Pictures of children in sexualised poses and in varying degree of nakedness.
- ***Explicit Erotic Posing:*** Pictures emphasising the genitals.
- ***Explicit Sexual Activity:*** Record of sexual activity involving children but not involving adult.
- ***Assault:*** Record of children subjected to sexual abuse involving digital touching with adults.
- ***Gross Assault:*** Record of children subjected to sexual abuse involving penetrative sex, masturbation, or oral sex with adults.
- ***Sadistic/Bestiality:*** Record of children subject to pain, or engaging in sexual activity with an animal.

The prepubescent pornography is viewed and collected by pedophiles for a variety of purposes, ranging from private sexual uses, trading with other pedophiles, preparing children for sexual abuse as part of the process known as "child grooming", or enticement leading to entrapment for sexual exploitation such as production of new child pornography or child prostitution.

Circulation Methods

The internet and advances in digital technology have provided fertile ground for offenders to obtain child pornography, share child pornography, produce child pornography, advertise child pornography and sell child pornography. The internet also has allowed offenders to form online communities with global membership not only to facilitate the trading and collection of these images but also to facilitate contact (with each other and children) and to create support network among offenders. Rather than simply downloading or uploading images of child pornography to and from the internet, offenders also use current technologies to talk about their sexual interest in children and to trade comments about the abuse depicted in particular images.

1. ***Web Pages and Websites:*** Specific child pornography websites may be created or child pornography image may be embedded in general pornography sites. There is an ongoing debate about how much child pornography is available on the web. Some argue that it is relatively easy to find images, while others argue that because of the vigilance of Internet Service Providers (ISPs) and police in tracking down and closing child pornography websites, it is unlikely that a normal web search using key word such as "childporn" would reveal much genuine child pornography. Instead, the search is likely to find legal pornographic sites with adults purporting to be minors, 'sting' operations, or vigilante sites.
2. ***Web Cam:*** Images of abuse may be broadcast in real time. In one documented case of a live broadcast, viewers could make online request for particular sexual activities to be carried out on the victim.
3. ***Email:*** Email attachment are sometimes used by professional distributors of child pornography, but more frequently they are used to share images among users, or sent to potential victims as part of the grooming/seduction process. This method is considered risky by seasoned users because of the danger in unwittingly sending email to undercover police posing as pedophiles or potential victims.
4. ***Chat Rooms:*** Chat rooms may be used to exchange child pornography and locate potential victims. Chat rooms may be password protected. Open chat rooms are avoided by seasoned child pornography because they are often infiltrated by undercover police.
5. ***Peer to Peer:*** Peer to peer networks facilitate file sharing among child pornography users. These networks permit closed groups to trade image.
6. ***E-groups:*** Specific child pornography e-groups also exist to permit members to receive and share pornographic images and exchange

information about new sites. Some of these groups appear on reputable servers and are swiftly shut down when they are detected. However, they may use code names or camouflage child pornography images among legal adult pornography to prolong their existence.

7. ***Newsgroups:*** Specific child pornography newsgroups provide members with a forum in which to discuss their sexual interest in children and to post-child pornography. This is one of the major methods of distributing child pornography. Some child pornography newsgroups are well-known to both users and authorities.

A Typology of Offending

As noted by Taylor and Quayle (2003), the internet provides the social, individual and technological circumstances in which an interest in child pornography flourished:

- ***Social:*** The internet has been used to create a self-justifying online community for child pornography users.
- ***Individual:*** Using the internet, individuals can access material and communicate with others through a computer terminal providing an apparently private sphere for the expression of sexual fantasy.
- ***Technological:*** Digital technology and the internet make it possible for child pornography consumers to become obsessive collectors so that the collection of images becomes an end in itself. The internet also provides a ready means to access material supporting increasingly extreme sexual fantasies. It can then be used to act out those fantasies with children in online interactions or in physical meeting arranged online.

Effects on the Children Portrayed

The vast majority of children who appear in child pornography have not been abducted or physically forced to participate. In most cases they know the producer — it may even be their father — and are manipulated into taking part by more subtle means. Nevertheless, to be the subject of child pornography can have devastating physical, social, and psychological effects on children. The children portrayed in child pornography are first victimised when their abuse is perpetrated and recorded. They are further victimised each time that record is accessed.

In one study, 100 victims of child pornography were interviewed about the effects of their exploitation—at the time it occurred and in later years. Referring to when the abuse was taking place, victims described the physical pain (e.g., around the genitals), accompanying somatic symptoms (such as headaches, loss of appetite, and sleeplessness), and feelings of psychological distress (emotional isolation, anxiety, and fear). However, most also felt a pressure to cooperate with the offender and not to disclose the offence, both out of loyalty to the offender and a sense of shame about their own behaviour. Only five cases were ultimately reported to authorities. In later years, the victims reported that initial feelings of shame and anxiety did not fade, but intensified to feelings of deep despair, worthlessness, and hopelessness. Their experience had provided them with a distorted model of sexuality, and many had particular difficulties in establishing and maintaining healthy emotional and sexual relationships.

Effects on Users

The effects of pornography on users have been extensively researched but results are contentious. There are at least five possible relationships between pornography use and the sexual abuse of children:

- ***Pornography Use is an Expression of Existing Sexual Interests:*** An individual who sexually abuses children seeks out child pornography as part of his/her pattern of sexual gratification. The offender's sexual interests cause his/her pornography use rather than the other way around.
- ***Pornography is Used to Prime the Individual to Offend:*** An individual deliberately views child pornography immediately prior to offending. Pornography is used in the short-term to sexually stimulate the offender in preparation for offending.
- ***Pornography has a Corrosive Effect:*** An individual becomes increasingly interested in child pornography, is attracted to images of increasing severity, and becomes desensitised to the harm victims experience. Use of pornography in the long-term may also increase the risk that the person will sexually abuse a child.
- ***Pornography has a Cathartic Effect:*** Viewing child pornography is the sole outlet for an individual's sexual attraction to children. Pornography use may substitute for, or even help the individual resist, engaging in hands-on offending.
- ***Pornography is a By-product of Pedophilia:*** Pornography is created in the process of carrying out sexual abuse or is used to

groom potential victims and prepare them for abuse. Pornography is incidental to the abuse suffered by the victim.

In all likelihood, the effects of child pornography vary among users, and all of the above relationships may apply depending upon the individual in question.

INDIAN LAWS

Child pornography in India is illegal. In February 2009, our Parliament has passed the "Information Technology Bill", banning the creation and transmission of child pornography. The Bill enables India's law enforcement agencies to take strict action against those seeking child pornography. For example, browsing for child pornography on the internet can lead to a 5-year term of imprisonment and ₹ 1 lakh fine.

In India, pornography is illegal. However, enforcement is extremely lax and pornographic materials are easily available in public places. Softcore and hardcore pornography movies/photos are easily accessible through magazines, films, or Internet. The law states that possessing and watching pornographic materials is legal, but production and distribution are prohibited. Pornographic films in India are referred to as Blue Films and are available virtually anywhere; especially in areas where pirated material is already being sold. Despite the illegality, stores selling X-rated material are abundant in major cities and advertise openly; laws are rarely enforced in this case. However, in 2010, Bombay High Court ruled that watching pornography is legal.

Section 67 of the Information Technology Act (ITA) deals with "publishing or transmitting obscene material in electronic form". The earlier Section in ITA was later widened as per ITA amendment 2009 in which child pornography and retention of records by intermediaries were all included. Publishing or transmitting obscene material in electronic form is dealt with here. Whoever publishes or transmits any material which is lascivious or appeals to the prurient interest or if its effect is such as to tend to deprave and corrupt persons who are likely to read the matter contained in it, shall be punished with first conviction for a term up to three years and fine of five lakh rupees and in second conviction for a term of five years and fine of ten lakh rupces or both. This Section is of historical importance since the landmark judgement in what is considered to be the first ever conviction under I.T. Act 2000 in India, was obtained in this Section in the famous case *State of Tamil Nadu* vs. *Suhas Katti* on 5 November, 2004. The strength of the Section and the reliability of electronic evidences were proved by the prosecution and conviction was brought about in this case, involving sending obscene message in the name of a married women amounting to cyber stalking, email spoofing and the criminal activity stated in this Section.

Section 67A deals with publishing or transmitting of material containing sexually explicit act in Electronic form. Contents of Section 67 when combined with the material containing sexually explicit material attract penalty under this Section. However, accessing "obscene" content privately is not illegal. The Information Technology Act was amended by the Parliament in 2009, and **Section 67B** was inserted which criminalises browsing, downloading, creation, and publishing child pornography. Child anime porn was not explicitly criminalised.

The Protection of Children from Sexual Offences Act 2012

The Protection of Children from Sexual Offences Act 2012 defines a child as any person below the age of 18 years and provides protection to all children under the age of 18 years from the offences of sexual assault, sexual harassment and pornography. These offences have been clearly defined for the first time in law. The Act provides for stringent punishments, which have been graded as per the gravity of the offence. The punishments range from simple to rigorous imprisonment of varying periods. There is also provision for fine, which is to be decided by the Court. An offence is treated as "aggravated" when committed by a person in a position of trust or authority of child such as a member of security forces, police officer, public servant, etc.

Punishments for Offences covered in the Act are:

- ***Penetrative Sexual Assault (Section 3)*** — Not less than seven years which may extend to imprisonment for life, and fine (Section 4).
- ***Aggravated Penetrative Sexual Assault (Section 5)*** — Not less than ten years which may extend to imprisonment for life, and fine (Section 6).
- ***Sexual Assault (Section 7)*** — Not less than three years which may extend to five years, and fine (Section 8).
- ***Aggravated Sexual Assault (Section 9)*** — Not less than five years which may extend to seven years, and fine (Section 10).
- ***Sexual Harassment of the Child (Section 11)*** — Three years and fine (Section 12).

- ***Use of Child for Pornographic Purposes (Section 13)*** — Five years and fine and in the event of subsequent conviction, seven years and fine [Section 14 (1)].

The Act provides for the establishment of **Special Courts** for trial of offences under the Act, keeping the best interest of the child as of paramount importance at every stage of the judicial process.

INTERNATIONAL CONVENTION

Laws regarding child pornography exist in 94 of 187 Interpol member states as of 2008. Of those 94 countries, 58 criminalised possession of child pornography regardless of intent to distribute. This figure does not count legislation outlawing all pornography as being specific to child pornography; figures also including non-specific bans on all pornography would, therefore, be higher if available. Convictions for possessing child pornography also usually include prison sentences, but those sentences are often converted to probation for first-time offenders. Some nations such as Canada and Australia have laws banning cartoon, manga or written child pornography and others require ISPs (Internet Service Provider) to monitor internet traffic to detect it.

The United Nations Optional Protocol on the Rights of the Child requires states to outlaw the "producing, distributing, disseminating, importing, exporting, offering, selling or possessing for the above purposes" of child pornography. The Council of Europe's Cybercrime Convention, and the EU Framework Decision that became active in 2006, require signatory or member states to criminalise all aspects of child pornography. Article 34 of the United Nations Convention on the Rights of the Child (UNCRC) stated that all signatories shall take appropriate measures to prevent the exploitative use of children in pornographic performances and materials.

Convention on the Rights of the Child

UNICEF's mission is to advocate for the protection of children's rights, to help meet their basic needs and to expand their opportunities to reach their full potential. UNICEF is guided in doing this by the provisions and principles of the Convention on the Rights of the Child.

Built on varied legal systems and cultural traditions, the Convention is a universally agreed set of non-negotiable standards and obligations. These basic standards — also called human rights — set minimum entitlements and freedoms that should be respected by Governments.

They are founded on respect for the dignity and worth of each individual, regardless of race, colour, gender, language, religion, opinions, origins, wealth, birth status or ability and, therefore, apply to every human being everywhere. With these rights comes the obligation on both Governments and individuals not to infringe on the parallel rights of others. These standards are both interdependent and indivisible; we cannot ensure some rights without — or at the expense of — other rights.

A Legally Binding Instrument

The Convention on the Rights of the Child is the first legally binding international instrument to incorporate the full range of human rights — civil, cultural, economic, political and social rights. In 1989, world leaders decided that children needed a special convention just for them because people under 18 years old often need special care and protection that adults do not. The leaders also wanted to make sure that the world recognised that children have human rights too.

The Convention sets out these rights in 54 articles and two Optional Protocols. It spells out the basic human rights that children everywhere have the right to survival; to develop to the fullest; to protection from harmful influences; abuse and exploitation; and to participate fully in family, cultural and social life. The four core principles of the Convention are non-discrimination; devotion to the best interests of the child; the right to life; survival and development; and respect for the views of the child. Every right spelled out in the Convention is inherent to the human dignity and harmonious development of every child. The Convention protects children's rights by setting standards in health care, education, legal, civil and social services.

By agreeing to undertake the obligations of the Convention (by ratifying or acceding to it), National Governments have committed themselves to protecting and ensuring children's rights and they have agreed to hold themselves accountable for this commitment before the international community. States parties to the Convention are obliged to develop and undertake all actions and policies in the light of the best interests of the child.

Children's Rights in the Human Rights Framework

The Convention on the Rights of the Child sets out the rights that must be realised for children to develop their full potential, free from hunger and want, neglect and abuse. It reflects a new vision of the child.

Children are neither the property of their parents nor are they helpless objects of charity. They are human beings and are the subject of their own rights. The Convention offers a vision of the child as an individual and as a member of a family and community, with rights and responsibilities appropriate to his or her age and stage of development. By recognising children's rights in this way, the Convention firmly sets the focus on the whole child.

The Convention and its acceptance by so many countries has heightened recognition of the fundamental human dignity of all children and the urgency of ensuring their well-being and development. The Convention makes clear the idea that a basic quality of life should be the right of all children, rather than a privilege enjoyed by a few.

Conclusion

Thus, it is evident that technological advances have contributed significantly to the overall increase in the child pornography threat. Offenders can easily produce child sex abuse images using digital technologies and distribute the images over the internet. Prior to the mid-1990, internet access and availability of digital home recording devices (still, video, and web camera) were very limited, thereby confining the production and distribution of child pornography material to relatively few individuals. Today, the ease with which a person can move from viewing child pornography to producing and distributing child pornography is illustrated in numerous cases. So, we should enforce national and international law strictly to combat online child pornography in order to protect children from abuse.

REFERENCES

Grant, A., David, F. and Grabosky, P., 1997. "Child Pornography in the Digital Age", in *Transnational Organised Crime*, Vol. 3, No. 4, pp. 171-88.

Information Technology Act, 2009.

Itzin, C., 1992. *Pornography: Women, Violence and Civil Liberty*, Oxford University Press.

Karlen, H. and Hagner, C., 1996. *Commercial Sexual Exploitation of Children in Some Eastern European Countries*, Bangkok, ECPAT.

Krone, Tony, 2004. "A Typology of Online Child Pornography Offending", *Trends and Issue in Crime and Criminal Justice*, Australian Institute of Criminology, Australia.

Sood, Geetika, 2010. "Internet Child Pornography Law in India", *Nyaya Deep*, New Delhi.

Taylor, M. and Quayle, E., 2003. *Child Pornography: An Internet Crime*, Hove: Brunner-Routledge.

The United Nations Optional Protocol on the Rights of the Child.

United Nations Convention on the Rights of the Child.

Woolak, J.; Mitchell, K. and Finkelhor, D., 2003. *Internet Sex Crime Against Minors: the Response of Law Enforcement*, New Hampshire: National Centre for Missing and Exploited Children, USA.

Websites

www.fbi.gov
www.missingkids.com
www.popcentre.org
www.unicef.org

7

FEMALE FOETICIDE

Introduction

Female foeticide is the act of aborting a foetus because it is female. The act of aborting or terminating a foetus while it is still in the womb, because it is female, is known as female foeticide. This can be done after determining the sex of the child before it is born, through ultrasound scan. Although, sex determination in India is illegal, the practice is rampant and has become a multi-million industry. Coupled with prospective parents desperate for a boy child, and physicians who are carrying out these abortions, female foeticide has become a shameful and shocking reality of our nation.

Reduction in Child Sex Ratio

According to a report of the United Nations Children's Fund (UNICEF), up to 50 million girls and women are missing from India's population as a result of systemic gender discrimination in. The data in Table 7.1 show that reduction of Child Sex Ratio (CSR) female per 1,000 males since 1991. The break-up of the country into the regions of the north-west, north-central, west, east and south offers a quick overview of the broad patterns in the last two decades.

At the national level, the decline of 18 points in 2001 has now been followed by a further decline of 13 points. To put it briefly, practices leading to fewer girls in the 0-6 age group have been spreading more thinly over the last decade over a much larger proportion of the country. The circle is widening. It was in 2001 that several states in north-west India witnessed plunges in their child sex ratios — with Punjab leading the way by dropping below the 800 mark, while other States such as Himachal Pradesh experienced huge declines for the first time. Secondly, 2001 made history because of evidence of child sex ratios falling below the 950 mark in the other parts of the country outside the north-west,

Table 7.1: Reduction in Child Sex Ratio (0-6 years) Census 1991, 2001 and 2011, Selected States

Sl.No.	*States*	*1991*	*2001*	*Difference 2001-1991*	*2011*	*Difference 2011-2001*
1.	North-West					
	Himachal Pradesh	951	896	−53	906	+10
2.	Punjab	875	798	−77	846	+48
3.	Haryana	879	819	−40	830	+11
4.	Chandigarh	899	845	−46	867	+22
5.	Delhi	915	868	−47	886	+2
6.	North-Central					
	Uttar Pradesh	928	916	−12	899	−17
7.	Madhya Pradesh	952	932	−20	912	−20
8.	West Gujarat	928	883	−45	886	+3
9.	Rajasthan	916	909	−7	883	−16
10.	Maharashtra	946	913	−33	883	−16
11.	Goa	964	938	−26	920	−18
12.	East Bihar	959	942	−17	933	−9
13.	Jharkhand	NA	965	—	943	−22
14.	West Bengal	967	960	−7	950	−10
15.	Nagaland	993	964	−29	944	−20
16.	Odisha	967	953	−14	934	−19
17.	South Andhra Pradesh	975	961	−14	943	−18
18.	Karnataka	960	946	−14	943	−3
19.	Tamil Nadu	948	942	−6	946	+4
20.	Kerala	958	960	+2	959	−1
	All India	**945**	**927**	**−18**	**914**	**−13**

Source: Compiled from Census of 2001 and Census of 2011.

such as Goa, urban Odisha and even pockets in the north-east. Moving on to Census 2011, the State figures point to a clear difference between the north-west and the rest of India. It would appear that there has been a peaking of the practice of sex selection in States like Gujarat, Haryana, Delhi and Himachal Pradesh, with small improvement from low levels in Chandigarh and Punjab. Punjab's rise from 798 to 846 (48 points) according to 2011 figures makes it now look more like its neighbours. The improvement has found in north-west India, CSRS are falling in large parts of western, central and eastern India. Thus, the state-wise figures demonstrate a widening of the circle-even if the numbers are not dramatic well beyond the so-called prosperity belt of north-west India, to the poorer state.

Historical Background

Female infanticide has been in practice since ancient times in the country.

There are some prone areas in the country where this practice is considered a part of their custom and tradition. Kolloor (1990) defines infanticide as "killing of an entirely dependent child under one year of age who is killed by mother, parents or others in whose care the child is entrusted." In recent years the misuse of ultrasound has reached remote tribal areas of Rajasthan, Bundelkhand and emerged even in other parts of India where women were better treated such as Assam, Kerala and the Kashmir Valley. The practice of female infanticide is documented to have existed in Europe in the early twentieth century and was found across Pakistan, West Asia, China and North Africa. The causes ascribed to that old practice include, besides the control of the population and socio-religious practices such as superstition and the disposal of handicapped/illegitimate babies, the gender-based selective killing of female children. One of the earliest records of female infanticide in India points to a clan of Rajputs in Uttar Pradesh, the discovery of which is credited to Jonathan Duncan, a British official posted in Northern India. Subsequent to this, the British Raj passed the Infanticide Regulation Act of 1870 to curb, among other variations, the widespread incidence of neonaticide (the killing of a baby within the first 24 hours of birth) (Singh, 2012).

Foeticide can be seen everywhere in India, and it has become more common with the advent and easy availability of technology, such as amniocentesis and sonography, that enables the determination of the gender of the foetus. Despite Government measures and laws against it, foeticide has not seen a decrease in its rate; on the contrary, it is increasing rapidly. The details of the cases of female infanticide are quite shocking. In Rajput families, "*doodh pilana*" is a common ritual reserved for newborn girls. Parents immerse the helpless child in a tub of milk until she chokes to death. In south Indian States like Tamil Nadu, children are either fed the milk of poisonous plants or covered with a wet towel, so that, they die later of complications from cold. In Bihar, holding the baby from the waist and shaking it back and forth snaps the spinal chord. Sometimes, a child is stuffed in a clay pot. Babies are also fed with salt to increase their blood pressure; death follows in a few minutes. Grains of paddy husk are also fed to slit the tender gullet. Furthermore, a change in the method of killing infants has been observed following the exhumation of bodies to get forensic evidence when it was suspected that an infant had been a victim of infanticide. People began to adopt methods such as starving the baby to death, which, unlike poisoning, leaves no forensic evidence as to the cause of death.

Causes of Female Foeticide

For centuries, families across many parts of India have regarded a male child as the preferred of the two sexes. There have been many social, financial, emotional and religious reasons for this preference and while times have changed, many of these reasons and beliefs continue to remain. The root cause of female foeticide is the *dowry* system in our society. A number of girls are killed inside the wombs due to fear of *dowry* in spite of having Dowry Prohibition Act 1961 and having penal laws under Section 304B of the Indian Penal Code. The poor family worried about giving dowry during the marriage of their girl child, which they cannot afford. According to Manu, a man has to be reborn as a man to attain '*moksha*' (redemption). A man cannot attain '*moksha*' unless he has a son to light his funeral pyre (Goswami, 2007:347). The age old preference for sons is motivated by economic, religious, social and emotional desires and norms that favour males and make female less desirable. Parents expect son, but not daughter to provide financial and emotional care, especially in their old age; sons add to family wealth and property while daughters drain it through dowries. The stereo type notion of women as 'burden' is one of the main reasons behind female foeticide. Today, some of the key reasons that exist for the preference of a male child are as follows:

- The tradition of paying dowry at the time of a daughter's marriage is alive and kicking. This amount can be so huge that many parents will go to extreme lengths to avoid having a daughter in the first place.
- A son can carry on the family name, while a daughter becomes part of her husband's family.
- The prevalent unhealthy social and family environment and the resultant social pressure, which affects women's thinking against women's dignity. It forces them to think that they are inferior beings, as compared to their brothers and thus anathematise their lives.
- Girls are seen as consumers, whereas boys are seen as producers.
- Many families consider it a status symbol to have a son, and a point of shame to have a daughter.
- A strong desire for sons is certainly associated with a religious faith to get salvation, if son lights the funeral pyre of his parents.
- Often, the pressure to bear a male child on the woman is so great that she herself might choose to get sex determination done and abort the baby if it is a girl.

- Illiteracy, poverty and the tag of 'burden' that is assigned to a girl child, makes the desire for a male child even stronger.
- Lack of education and awareness has also prompted female foeticide.

Modern technology has made it very easy to determine the sex of the child while it is still in the womb, giving parents the option of aborting the foetus and continuing to try to conceive till they get a male child. While sex determination has been banned by the Indian Government, it does not stop families from going to great lengths to find out anyway. Not only are there plenty of scanning centres that reveal this information, many of the wealthier families fly the pregnant mother to neighbouring countries where sex determination is legal, to find out the gender of the baby. Once the gender of the baby is known, families that are keen to have a baby boy choose to abort the female foetus. The law on aborting is also strict, and the Indian Government allows it only under certain circumstances.

The traditional value system of Indian society, sex segregation, poverty and the growing problem of dowries — all these have created an atmosphere where females are often considered a nuisance. The result is a declining child sex ratio in succeeding census reports. The mentality and attitudinal problem at the level of society are directly responsible for occurrence of such gaps in the society leading to various kinds of other problems in the forms of violence, rape, foeticide, infanticide, marginalisation, powerless, exploitation, cultural imperialism and traditional notion of polyandrous marriages to women of our contemporary society. (Iyer, 1979:31) has aptly remarked: "The fight is not for women's status but for human worth. The claim is not to end inequality of women but to restore universal justice. The bid is not for loaves and fishes for the forsaken gender but for cosmic harmony, which never comes till woman comes."

Statutory Protection Given Against Female Foeticide

The Government has also taken into consideration the gravity of the problem and enacted legislation to curb it. Maharashtra was the first State to ban the pre-netal sex determination through the enactment of the Maharashtra Regulation of Parental Diagnostic Technique Act. Similarly, at the national level the Central Pre-natal Diagnostic Techniques (Prohibition of Sex Selection) Act 1994 was enacted to prevent female foeticide (Agarwal, 2010:75). The purpose was to limit the use of pre-natal diagnostic techniques to genuine medical purpose and to prevent its misuse. It was amended and replaced in 2002 by the Pre-natal Diagnostic Techniques (Regulation and Prevention of Misuse) Act. The provisions are:

(i) The Act provides for the prohibition of sex selection, before or after conception.

(ii) The Act also regulates the use of pre-natal diagnostic techniques like ultrasound and amniocentesis by allowing them their use only to detect:

 (a) Genetic abnormalities,
 (b) Metabolic disorders,
 (c) Chromosomal abnormalities,
 (d) Certain congenital malformations,
 (e) Haemoglobinophathies, and
 (f) Sex linked disorders.

(iii) No laboratory or centre or clinic will conduct any test including ulrasonography for the purpose of determining the sex of the foetus.

(iv) No person, including the one who is conducting the procedure as per the law, will communicate the sex of the foetus to the pregnant woman or her relatives by words, sign or any other method.

(v) Any person who puts an advertisement for pre-natal and pre-conception sex determination facilities in the form of a notice, circular, label, wrapper or any document, or advertises through interior or other media in electronic or print form or engages on any visible representation made by means of hoarding, wall painting, signal, light, sound smoke or gas, can be imprisoned for up to three years and fines ₹ 10,000.

(v) *Punishment:* Further, provision has also been made that, suspension of the registration if the charges are framed by the court and till the case is disposed of and on conviction for removal of his name from the register of the Council for a period of five years for the first offence and permanently for the subsequent offence.

The Act has two aspects, viz. regulatory and preventive. It seeks to regulate the use of pre-natal diagnostic techniques for legal or medical purposes and to prevent misuse for illegal purpose. The Act provides for the setting up of various bodies along with their composition powers and functions. There is Central Supervisory Board, appropriate authorities and advisory committees. Of course, the Act plays very vital role in controlling derogatory practices of Medical Practitioners but at the same time its adverse advantages also taken by the miscreant of the society.

The Medical Termination of Pregnancy (MTP) Act 1971

MTP Act legalises abortion only in certain circumstances —

(a) Danger to the life of the mother in the child birth,
(b) If the child is at risk of being born handicapped, or
(c) Of the women has conceived the child as a result of rape. As a matter of fact, people in general is particularly avoided the provisions of the Act and the practice if female foeticide went on.

NOVEL AND INNOVATIVE PROGRAMME

Beti Bacho, Beti Padhao

Child Sex Ratio (CSR), defined as number of girls per 1000 of boys between 0-6 years of age, has been on decline in India since 1961 — from 945 in 1991 to 927 in 2001, and further to 919 in 2011. A 2012 UNICEF Report ranked India 41st among 195 countries. Haryana has the worst sex ratio among all States in the country, standing at just 879 females per 1000 males. Keeping in mind this skewed figure, Prime Minister Narendra Modi launched the '*Beti Bachao, Beti Padhao*' programme nation-wide on January 22, 2015 from Panipat in Haryana, to address the declining child sex ratio and empower girl child in the country. This programme will be implemented through a national multimedia campaign and focused multi-sectoral actions in 100 selected districts, low in Child Sex Ratio (CSR), covering all States and Union Territories. Further it has been decided by the Union Government that Ministry of Women and Child Development shall be the nodal Ministry for implementing in collaboration with the Ministry of Health and Family Welfare and Ministry of Human Resource Development.

The Objectives of this Scheme are:

- Prevent gender biased sex selective elimination.
- Ensure survival and protection of girl child.
- Ensure education of the girl child.

Strategies for Implementation

- To implement a sustained social mobilisation and communication campaign to create equal value for the girl child and promote her education.
- Place the issue of decline in Child Sex Ratio (CSR)/Sex Ratio at Birth (SBR) in public discourse, improvement of which would be an indicator for good governance.
- Focus on Gender Critical District and Cities, low on CSR for intensive and integrated action.
- Mobilise and train Panchayati Raj Institutions/Union Local Bodies/Grassroots workers as catalysts for social change, in partnership with local community/women's/youth groups.
- Ensure service delivery structures/schemes and programmes are sufficiently responsive to issues of gender and children's rights.
- Enable inter-sectoral and inter-institutional convergence at District/Block/Grassroots level.

Targets for Accomplishment

- Improve the SRB in 100 gender critical districts by 10 points in a year.
- Reduce gender differentials in Under Five Child Mortality Rate from 8 points in 2011 to 4 points by 2017.
- Improve the Nutrition status of girls by reducing number of underweight and anaemic girls less than 5 years of age.
- Ensure universalisation of ICDS, girls' attendance and equal are monitored, using ICDS-NRHM Mother Child Protection Cards.
- Increase the girls' enrollment in secondary education from 76 per cent in 2013-14 to 79 per cent by 2017.
- Provide girls' toilet in every school in 100 CSR districts by 2017.
- Promote a protective environment for girl children through implementation of Protection of Children from Sexual Offences (POCSO) Act 2012.
- Train Elected Representative/Grassroots functionaries as Community Champions to mobilise communities to improve CSR and promote girls' education.

Significant Section of Programme

The *Beti Bachao, Beti Padhao* (BBBP) initiative has two major components:

Media Campaign: The campaign will be aimed at ensuring girls are born, nurtured and educated without discrimination to become empowered citizens of this country with equal rights. The campaign will interlink National, State and District level interventions with community level action in 100 districts, bringing together different stakeholders for accelerated impact.

Multi-Sectoral Action in 100 Selected Districts (as a pilot) with Adverse CSR, Covering all States and UTs: Multi-Sectoral actions include measurable outcomes and indicators which will bring together concerned sectors, states and districts for urgent rigorous multi-sectoral action to improve the CSR. The States/UTs will adapt a flexible framework for multi-sectoral action through the State Task Forces for developing, implementing and monitoring State/District Plans of Action to achieve the State/District Specific Monitorable Targets (Ganguli, 2015:39).

The Role of Judiciary

The Supreme Court observed in *Centre for Enquiry into Health and Allied Themes (CEHAT) & Others* vs. *Union of India & Others* on 4th May, 2001: "It is unfortunate that for one reason or the other, the practice of female infanticide still prevails despite the fact that gentle touch of a daughter and her voice has soothing effect on the parents. One of the reasons may be the marriage problems faced by the parents coupled with the dowry demand by the so-called educated and/or rich persons who are well placed in the society. The traditional system of female infanticide whereby female baby was done away with after birth by poisoning or letting her choke on husk continues in a different form by taking advantage of advance medical techniques. Unfortunately, developed medical science is misused to get rid of a girl child before birth. Knowing fully well that it is immoral and unethical as well as it may amount to an offence; foetus of a girl child is aborted by qualified and unqualified doctors or compounders. This has affected overall sex ratio in various States where female infanticide is prevailing without any hindrance."

The law exists for the well-being of the people in the society, but the same law can sometimes be misused at the same time in the name of this well-being, by the people. The enactment of the law in the form of the Medical Termination of Pregnancy Act from 1974 declared abortion legal under certain conditions during the first trimester of pregnancy. To ensure proper implementation of this law in an era of technological advancement, much consideration has been given this law by the Apex Court of the country.

Coming down heavily on doctors carrying out sex determination tests, the Allahabad High Court has said that the law against it has not been effectively enforced in States like Uttar Pradesh. "The number of deaths of female children in the womb (female foeticide) in the last decade has exceeded the total deaths in the First and the Second World War", a Division Bench comprising Justices Sunil Ambwani and Manoj Kumar Gupta said in a judgement dated May 17, 2013. "It is unfortunate that in a civilized country like India some people, for their petty gains, are using modern technology for sex determination which ultimately leads to abortion of female foetus", the Court said, adding it was "pained to observe" that many "qualified and registered doctors" were involved in such practices.

The Court expressed dismay over the fact that in the last one decade, doctors in the country "have been responsible for abortions of 10 million women, killing female children in the womb. This mass carnage of female foetuses in womb has made Indian doctors responsible for the crime which has no parallel in the history of modern medical science." The Court expressed dissatisfaction over the fact that though the PNDT Act was in force, it was not being effectively implemented especially in States like Uttar Pradesh where "effective steps to seal the clinics and prosecute the doctors" has not been taken. The observations were made while dismissing the writ petition of Dr. Dwarika Prasad from Kushinagar district of Uttar Pradesh, who had challenged the District Magistrate's order dated March 16, 2013 whereby the licence of his Ultrasound and X-ray centre was cancelled for violating the PNDT Act. The Court upheld the order of the District Magistrate observing that he had done a "commendable job" and directed him to "refer the petitioner's case to the Medical Council of India" for further action, besides ordering that criminal proceedings be initiated against him for carrying out sex determination tests. In a recent landmark judgment the Mumbai High Court upheld an amendment to the PNDT Act banning sex selection treatment. The Court pronounced that pre-natal sex determination would be as good as female foeticide. Pre-conception sex determination violated a woman's right to live and was against the Constitution, it said.

Suggestions

Government rules and regulations are not sufficient to eradicate female foeticide from the society. The long-term solution is to change the attitude of the people. Government agencies, civil society and media should work hand in hand to combat this problem.

- There should be registration of all nursing homes and rigorous action should be taken against the defaulters.
- The administration should be made accountable for low male-female ratios in their area.
- Government should aware the people about the importance of girls and should not consider them as stigma to their families.
- Proper measures should be taken to implement anti-dowry law and culprits should be punished.
- There is need to remove the myth of son preference from our society only then this problem can be tackled.
- Doctors must also be sensitised and strong punitive measures must be taken against those who violate the law.
- Volunteers have to be actively mobilised to monitor the registration and the functioning of the sex-determination clinics.
- Inculcation of education and awareness is a necessary step. A lesson on gender equity should be included in school curriculum.

Conclusion

Female Foeticide, is a gross violation of basic human right guaranteed under Article 21 of the Constitution of India. In the case of female foeticide, the female children in the wombs of expecting mothers, they are not only denied the right to live but are robbed to their right to be born. The selection of male child over female is enough proof for lack of right to birth to girl child. Social, cultural, financial and psychological reasons are responsible for the prevalence of evil female foeticide in our society. Unfortunately, it became popular for sex determination, leading to sex selective abortions for those who do not want to be burdened with female child. The more easy way was shown by Medical Termination of Pregnancy Act 1971 by legalising abortions in certain specific conditions and ultimately became a tool for female sex-selective abortions and led to drastic fall in the female sex ratio to present level. Male child preference is a pivotal factor in female foeticide. The normative preference for the male child emanates from gender typed roles, male inheritance and decadence. In our society people think that male child brings social status for them. All religions have legitimised gender inequalities and accorded an inferior status to women. Manu, the Hindu Law Giver, denied autonomy to women, and advised that women should be guarded day and night. Science has made this a less messy procedure through female foeticide. Dowry system is alsó crucial in preventing the birth of a girl child. Girl child is treated as a bird of passage, a guest in her own parent's house. Small family norm is also responsible for female foeticide. Middle class families prefer norm of two-child family. Decrease in family size ensured the survival of male child at the cost of female child. This norm has displaced the girl child. The practice of sex determination followed by abortion in case of female child is not only illegal but constitutes a criminal offence. It was proposed to prohibit pre-natal diagnostic techniques for determination of sex of foetus for the purpose of female foeticide. Such abuse of scientific technique was found discriminatory against female sex and also affecting the dignity and status of women. Law alone cannot stop the social evil of female foeticide, but it needs social awareness and active role of media. The gravity of problem demands immediate measures to combat female foeticide. Mere legal enactments and provisions under the Constitution of India with the purpose of safeguarding the rights of women and children will not serve their purpose until the mindset and attitudes of people change. The growing problem of missing girls and declining child sex ratio will impede human development towards full gender parity. Thus, everyone has a stake in helping to overcome these destructive and regressive customs. Social scientists, medical practitioners, common men, judicial officials, legal professionals and NGOs all need to focus on a humanist and scientific approach. There is a need for a strong ethical code for medical practitioners.

REFERENCES

Agarwal, Sivani, 2010. "A Social Menace — Female Foeticide", *Nyaya Deep*, October, pp, 72-77.

Bajpayee, Asha, 2003. *Child Rights in India*, Oxford University Press, New Delhi.

Bhat, P. Ishwara, 2009. *Law and Social Transformation*, EBC, Lucknow.

Ceetu, Sengeeta, 1991. "Growing Menace of Female Foeticide in India", *Indian Socio-Legal Journal*, Vol. xvii(1).

Ganguli, Barna, 2015. "Empowering Women", *Kurukshetra*, March, Vol. 63. No. 5.

Goswami, Sambodh, 2007. *Female Infanticide and Child Marriage*, Rawat Publication, Jaipur.

Iyer, V.K. Krishna, 1979. *Of Law and Life*, Vikas Publishing House, New Delhi.

Jena, K.C., 2012. "Female Foeticide and Infanticide in India: The Emerging Issues", *Indian Bar Council Review*, Vol. XXXIX(1).

John, E. Mary, 2011. "Census 2011: Governing Population and the Girl Child", *Economic and Political Weekly*, April 16, Vol. XLVI, No. 16.

Kolloor, T.M., 1990. "Female Infanticide: A Psychological Analysis", *Grass Roots Action*, Special Issue on Girl Child, 3 April.

Misra, Dipak, 2007. "Female Foeticide — A Social Menace", *Nyaya Deep*, April, Vol. VIII, Issue 2, pp. 25-34.

Patil, Tejaswini, 2012. "Save Babies . . . . Save Doctors", *Indian Bar Review*, Vol. XXXIX(4).

PNDT Act 2002.

Sarkar, Pratim, 2013. "Women Killing Practice in India and the Legal Concern", *Law Profile*, June, Vol. 4, Issue 6.

Singh, Bir Pal, 2012. "Sociology of Female Foeticide and Infanticide. Where does the Law Stand?", *Gender Forum — An Internet Journal for Gender Studies*, Issue 38.

The Dowry Prohibition Act 1961.

The Medical Termination of Pregnancy (MTP) Act 1971.

Website

https://en.wikipedia.org/wiki/Female_Foeticide_in_India

8

CHILD MARRIAGE

Introduction

Child marriage is a formal marriage or informal union before the age of 18. While child marriage is observed for both boys and girls, overwhelming majority are girls. Child marriage most often occurs in poor, rural communities. Child marriage in India has been practiced for centuries, with children married off before their physical and mental maturity. The problem of child marriage in India remains rooted in a complex matrix of religious traditions, social practices, economic factors and deeply rooted prejudices. Regardless of its roots, child marriage constitutes a gross violation of human rights, leaving physical, psychological and emotional scars for life. Sexual activity starts soon after marriage, and pregnancy and child birth at an early age. The Government of India enacted the Child Marriage Restraint Act (Amended) in 1978 and raised the age at marriage for girls from 15 to 18 and for boys 18 to 21 years, in spite of this legislation child marriages still prevail in India on account of poor implementation by the Government machinery and lack of knowledge about the legislation among the parents. Moreover, socio-cultural and economic factors also support the continuance of this practice, child marriage may not have an immediate impact on fertility, but it certainly influences the girls' individual development like her education, health, socialisation and so on. Child marriage mostly takes place with the kin group, rational behind such marriage is to maintain and strengthen the clan lineage.

UNICEF defined child marriage, as a formal marriage or informal union before age 18, is a reality for both boys and girls, although girls are disproportionately the most affected. About a third of women aged 20-24 years old in the developing world were married as children. Child marriage is most common in South Asia and Sub-Saharan Africa, but there are big differences in prevalence among countries of the same region. While data from 47 countries show that, overall, the median age at first marriage is gradually increasing, this improvement has been limited primarily to girls of families with higher incomes. Overall, the pace of change remains slow. While 48 per cent of women 45-49 years old were married before the age of 18, the proportion has only dropped to 35 per cent of women 20-24 years old (UNICEF, 2010). Evidence shows that girls who marry early often abandon formal education and become pregnant. Maternal deaths related to pregnancy and childbirth are an important component of mortality for girls aged 15-19 worldwide, accounting for 70,000 deaths each year (UNICEF, 2009). If a mother is under the age of 18, her infant's risk of dying in its first year of life is 60 per cent greater than that of an infant born to a mother older than 19. Even if the child survives, he or she is more likely to suffer from low birth weight, under nutrition and late physical and cognitive development. Child brides are at risk of violence, abuse and exploitation. Finally, child marriage often results in separation from family and friends and lack of freedom to participate in community activities, which can all have major consequences on girls' mental and physical well-being. Where prevalent, child marriage functions as a social norm (UNICEF, 2009). Marrying girls under 18 years old is rooted in gender discrimination, encouraging premature and continuous child bearing and giving preference to boys' education. Child marriage is also a strategy for economic survival as families marry off their daughters at an early age to reduce their economic burden.

UNICEF works with communities to raise the age of marriage and address gender discrimination through awareness raising and community discussions at local and national levels and assists governments in strengthening national legislation, policies and services.

Child marriage is a common practice in many countries around the world, however, it is especially prevalent in India, where more than one-third of all child brides live. According to UNICEF, 47 per cent of girls are married by 18 years of age, and 18 per cent are married by 15 years of age. These marriages are often performed without the consent of the girls involved in the marriage. Indian Law has made child marriage illegal, but it is still widely practiced across the nation. The highest rates are seen particularly in the rural States of Andhra Pradesh, Telengana, Bihar, Madhya Pradesh, Rajasthan and Uttar Pradesh. It affects both boys and girls, but statistics show that girls are far more likely to be forced into a child marriage than boys; however, the percentage of girls forced into child marriage in India has declined in recent years.

The first-ever U.N. Human Rights Council resolution against the practice of child, early and forced marriages has already been co-sponsored by 107 other countries on multiple continents. India, however, refused to sponsor the measure stating that the resolution's definition of early marriage was vague. Although the legal age for marriage in India is 18, its 24 million underage child brides constitute nearly half of all child brides in the world. The resolution as floated by the UN Human Rights Council has stressed the need to include child, early and forced marriage in post-2015 international development agenda and acknowledged the impact of early marriage on the "economic, legal, health and social status of women and girls" as well as "the development of the community as a whole" (*The Hindu*, 2013).

Causes for Child Marriage

- Children are married young to ensure their obedience and subservience within the family.
- Child marriage is also soleminised because people have their own ideas of fertility and childbearing capacity. Early marriage ensures full utilisation of this capacity.
- The feudal background of the state restricted access of education to masses, especially for girls. The prevailing gender biases prevented a girl child from acquiring any other skills except those complementing her biological capacity. Such biases and values favour early marriage.
- The economic reason also has contributed in the acceptance and continuance of this practice.
- Marrying children is considered an important duty by the parents and an important obligation for the attainment of *moksha*. People believe that religious scriptures prescribe early marriages for children and they try to do this at the earliest available opportunity.
- Tremendous pressure from older members of the Indian society like grandparents and also the community prevails on parents of children to marry off their young children. There is also the fear of not getting the suitable match if the marriage is delayed.

Impact of Child Marriage

Child marriage is a truly global problem that cuts across countries, cultures, religions and ethnicities. In 2010, 13.5 million girls were married before they turned 18. If we do nothing, by 2030 an estimated 15.4 million girls a year will marry as children. In the developing world, one in seven girls is married before her 15th birthday and some child brides are as young as eight or nine. Neither physically nor emotionally ready to become wives and mothers, these girls are at far greater risk of experiencing dangerous complications in pregnancy and childbirth, becoming infected with HIV/AIDS. With little access to education and economic opportunities, they and their families are more likely to live in poverty.

World Health Organization declares, there are multiple consequences of child marriage in terms of the health, social and economic situation of adolescent girls. Early onset of sexual activity and the pressure on young married women to prove their fertility as soon as possible after marriage results in high rates of fertility. Child Marriages usually have profound adverse effects on the fertility, health and development of adolescent girls, low age of marriage is one of the important factors responsible for the high rates of maternal and child mortality and morbidity (Jejeebhoy, 1999).

High fertility rate is attributed to an early marriage, i.e. child marriage. The earlier a time a woman marries the more likely she is to give birth to a larger number of children, consequently placing a high demand on her health (Bhat, 2005). Early pregnancy, therefore, has a tendency to lead to larger families, with serious consequences for the health and well-being of the mother as well as her children. In addition to its harmful effects on the health of mothers and children, this phenomenon has universal implications for populations at large.

Child marriage also results in the trafficking of children for various purposes, including prostitution, labour and exploitation. Young girls are lured/forced into marriage for the purpose of selling them to other states. Studies in child trafficking have shown that child marriage is used as a legal instrument for committing illegal trafficking. A study conducted by HAQ (Centre for child rights), showed that girls from West Bengal were trafficked to remote regions such as Kashmir. A large number of girls were being trafficked from Bengal to J&K mainly for the purpose of marrying them to older men or forcing them into prostitution after marriage.

A UNICEF study points out that India has one of the highest levels of domestic violence whereby 67 per cent of women, who were married less than 18 years faced domestic violence. It has the highest levels of domestic violence cases among women compared to other countries like

Zambia, South Africa, Cambodia, etc. (UNICEF, 2005). Domestic violence is a major problem among adolescent girls who marry early. Women who marry younger are more likely to be beaten, threatened or sexually abused.

Role of *Khap* Panchayat

Haryana's *Sarva Khap Jat Panchayat* is now discussing the bizarre suggestion that the marriage age for girls be lowered to curb rising incidents of rape in the State. The supreme council is an umbrella body of *khap panchayats* across the State. *Khaps* have no legal sanction, but often function like *kangaroo* courts and issue social *diktats* that are enforced in the villages.

A meeting called in Sonepat, about 40 km from Delhi, to discuss the marriage age issue and how the Government could be compelled to get the bar lowered in Haryana, where at least 15 rapes have been reported."The meeting aims at knowing the views of various *khap panchayats* about the issue of lowering the marriageable age to prevent rape incidents in the State. Representatives of around 100 *khaps* across the State had attended the meeting to share their opinion and to present their proposals on the issue," Sube Singh Samain, spokesperson of the *Sarva Khap Jat Panchayat*, said. Sube Singh had suggested that lowering the marriage age for women would prevent rape. He found backing from Indian National Lok Dal leader and former Haryana Chief Minister Om Prakash Chautala who said: "I am with the *khaps* on this issue. This will protect women."

Randhir Singh, Chief of the *Sarva Khap Panchayat Meham Chaubisi* (which represents 24 villages of Meham sub-division in Rohtak), said that the Government should not only remove the existing restriction on the marriageable age, but leave the decision on a girl's parents. Under the law, girls below 18 years and boys below 21 years cannot legally get married."Let the parents decide when they want to marry off their wards. Girls can be married off a couple of years earlier than the stipulated age of 18 years if they have physically grown up," Randhir Singh said. The view has been met with outrage. Jagmati Sangwan, national vice president of the Janwadi Mahila Samiti, said: "There is no direct relation between rape and the marriageable age."

Hence, the suggestion cannot be described as appropriate. Besides, other precautionary measures, bringing about a change in the mentality of the people is also required to check crimes against women. Jagjit Dagar, district president of the Haryana Janhit Congress, Youth Wing, said: "The suggestion is entirely wrong and it will give a boost to social evils. The Government should make some serious efforts for the security and safety of women in the State."

LEGAL PERSPECTIVE OF CHILD MARRIAGE

There are three laws dealing with child marriage in India: The Child Marriage (Restaint) Act 1929, The Prevention of Child Marriage Act 2004, Prohibition of Child Marriage Act 2006. Compulsory Registration of Marriage Act 2006.

Some of the important features of Prohibition of Child Marriage Act 2006, are —

- Every child marriage, whether solemnised before or after the commencement of this Act, shall be voidable at the option of the contracting party who was a child at the time of the marriage.
- While granting a decree under Section 3, the district court may also make an interim or final order directing the male contracting party to the child marriage, and in case the male contracting party to such marriage is a minor, his parent or guardian to pay maintenance to the female contracting party to the marriage until her remarriage.
- Where there are children born of the child marriage, the district court shall make an appropriate order for the custody of such children.
- Notwithstanding that a child marriage has been annulled by a decree of nullity under Section 3, every child begotten or conceived of such marriage before the decree is made, whether born before or after the commencement of this Act, shall be deemed to be a legitimate child for all purpose.
- The district court shall have the power to add to, modify or revoke any order made under Section 4 or Section 5 and if there is any change in the circumstance at any time during the pendency of the petition and even after the final disposal of the petition.
- Whoever, being a male adult above eighteen years of age, contracts a child marriage shall be punishable with rigorous imprisonment which may extend to two years or with fine which may extend to one lakh rupees or with both.
- Whoever performs, conducts, directs or abets any child marriage shall be punishable with rigorous imprisonment which may extend to two years and shall be liable to fine which may extend to one

lakh rupees unless he proves that he had reasons to believe that the marriage was not a child marriage.

- Any child marriage solemnised in contravention of an injunction order issued under Section 13, whether interim or final, shall be *void ab initio.*
- Notwithstanding anything contained in the Code of Criminal Procedure, 1973, an offence punishable under this Act shall be cognizable and non-bailable.
- The State Government shall, by notification in the Official Gazette, appoint for the whole State, or such part thereof as may be specified in the notification, an officer or officers to be known as the Child Marriage Prohibition Officer having jurisdiction over the area or area specified in the notification.

Compulsory Registration of Marriage Act 2006

From the year 2006, all marriages need to be registered in India under Compulsory Registration of Marriage Act 2006. It states that every Indian citizen needs to register his or her marriage within ten days of their marriage, irrespective of religion. Such compulsory registration would be of critical importance to prevent child marriage in the country. The Central Government has made it mandatory for all States to make registration of marriage compulsory saying that the State are in a better position to know the social structure and local condition about their respective State.

GOVERNMENT POLICIES

To fight with the menace of child marriage, Government of India has initiated number of policies and programmes, which are —

National Charter for Children, 2003

The State and community shall ensure that crimes and atrocities committed against the girl child, including child marriage, discriminatory practices, forcing girls into prostitution and trafficking are speedily eradicated. The State shall in partnership with the community undertake measures, including social, educational and legal, to ensure that there is greater respect for the girl child in the family and society. The State shall take serious measures to ensure that the practice of child marriage is speedily abolished.

The State recognises the common responsibilities of both parents in rearing their children. Every child has a right to a family. In case of separation of children from their families, the State shall ensure the priority is given to re-unifying the child with its parents. In cases where the State perceives adverse impact of such a re-unification, the State shall make alternate arrangements immediately, keeping in mind the best interests and the views of the child.

Kishori Shakti Yojana

Kishori Shakti Yojana (KSY) seeks to empower adolescent girls, so as to enable them to take charge of their lives. It is viewed as a holistic initiative for the development of adolescent girls. The programme through its interventions aims at bringing about a difference in the lives of the adolescent girls. It seeks to provide them with an opportunity to realise their full potential. This scheme is a redesign of the already existing Adolescent Girls (AG) Scheme being implemented as a component under the Centrally Sponsored Integrated Child Development Services (ICDS) Scheme. The new scheme dramatically extends the coverage of the earlier scheme with significant content enrichment, strengthens the training component, particularly in skill development, aspects aimed at empowerment and enhanced self-perception. It also fosters convergence with other sectoral programmes, addressing the interrelated needs of adolescent girls and women. The broad objectives of the Scheme are to improve the nutritional, health and development status of adolescent girls, promote awareness of health, hygiene, nutrition and family care, link them to opportunities for learning life skills, going back to school, help them gain a better understanding of their social environment and take initiatives to become productive members of the society.

Balika Samriddhi Yojana

The objective of Balika Samriddhi Yojana is to change negative family and community attitudes towards the girl child at birth and towards her mother. It also tries to improve enrollment, retention of girl children in schools and assist the girl to undertake income generating activities. It will cover both rural and urban areas in all districts in India. The Balika Samriddhi Yojana will cover girl children in families Below the Poverty Line (BPL) as defined by the Government of India, in rural and urban areas, who are born on or after 15 August, 1997.

(i) In rural areas the target group can be taken as the families which have been identified to be below the poverty line in accordance with the norms specified under Swarnajayanti Gram Swarojgar Yojana (known as such with effect from 1.4.1999), previously known as Integrated Rural Development Programme (IRDP).

(ii) In urban areas, wherever household surveys have been conducted as per the instructions of Government of India and lists of BPL families are prepared, such lists can be used. Wherever such lists are not prepared, the list of families covered under the Targetted Public Distribution System (TPDS) may be followed. Where neither of these lists are available, as a rule of thumb, families living in urban slums, both recognised as well as those not recognised, may be covered. Also, families which are in urban informal sector and working as rag-pickers, vegetable/fish and flower sellers, pavement dwellers, etc. would also be eligible. Applications may also be collected from families in non-slum areas.

Benefits under BSY will be restricted to two girl children in each household born on or after 15 August, 1997 irrespective of the total number of children in the household.

National Policy for the Empowerment of Women, 2001

The goal of this Policy is to bring about the advancement, development and empowerment of women. The Policy will be widely disseminated so as to encourage active participation of all stakeholders for achieving its goals. Specifically, the objectives of this Policy include —

(i) Creating an environment through positive economic and social policies for full development of women to enable them to realise their full potential.

(ii) The *de jure* and *de facto* enjoyment of all human rights and fundamental freedom by women on equal basis with men in all spheres — political, economic, social, cultural and civil.

(iii) Equal access to participation and decision-making of women in social, political and economic life of the nation.

(iv) Equal access to women to health care, quality education at all levels, career and vocational guidance, employment, equal remuneration, occupational health and safety, social security and public office, etc.

(v) Strengthening legal systems aimed at elimination of all forms of discrimination against women.
(vi) Changing societal attitudes and community practices by active participation and involvement of both men and women.
(vii) Mainstreaming a gender perspective in the development process.
(viii) Elimination of discrimination and all forms of violence against women and the girl child.
(ix) Building and strengthening partnerships with civil society, particularly women's organisations.

Girl Child Protection Scheme, 2005

The main objectives underlying this scheme includes elimination of prejudice against the girl child through direct investment from the Government, encouraging enrollment of the girl child in school and to ensure her education at least up to the Intermediate level and to get married only after the age of 18 years (which is the prescribed statutory limit). It also aims to reduce the school drop-out rate among the girls and to encourage parents to adopt family planning norms with two girl children. Other objectives are as follows:

- To provide social and financial empowerment to the girl child.
- Eliminating all forms of discrimination against the girl child.
- Providing social and financial empowerment to the girl child.
- Removing negative cultural attitudes and practices against girls.
- Promoting and protecting the rights of the girl child and to increase awareness of her needs and potential.

Government programmes are also effective in these fields which are: Reproductive Child Health Programme, Integrated Population Development Programme, Women Development Programme, Adolescent Girls Scheme, Nehru Yuvak Kendra Sangathan, National Service Schemes, etc.

Along with Government policies and programmes the grassroots level Non-Governmental Organisations (NGOs) have played an important role in working on various social issues. NGOs are close to the communities they serve and can, therefore, identify and respond appropriately to community needs and implement effective interventions to change social norms and risk-taking behaviour.

Free Education for Girls

Most of the parents are unable to give education to girl child due to financially bad condition. As a result, the girls are deprived from education and are not able to achieve desirable status in family, social, educational, financial and in political field. It also affects girls education in next generation and as such social change from female angle is not achieved. Therefore, Central Government had started the scheme of giving "Free Education for Girls" from standard first to twelve from 1st June, 1985. The scheme is implemented without any income obligation. The scheme is applicable to Primary, Secondary and Higher Secondary Schools/ Junior Colleges of State Government, Zilla Parishad, Municipal Corporation, Nagar Palika. Also, girls in Private recognised Aided Schools and Non-aided Institutes (which are charging Government determined Education fees) which runs Primary, Secondary and Higher Secondary Schools/Junior Colleges are eligible for benefit under the scheme.

Recommendations

- Education is one of the most powerful tools to delay the age at which girls marry as school attendance helps shift norms around child marriage.
- Improving girls' access to quality schooling will increase girls' chances of gaining a secondary education and helps to delay marriage.
- When a girl in the developing world receives seven or more years of education, she marries on average four years later.
- Empowering girls, by offering them opportunities to gain skills and education, providing support networks and creating 'safe spaces' where girls can gather and meet outside the home, can help girls to assert their right to choose when they marry.
- Rectifying the loopholes in the law is a significant way to control child marriages.
- All stakeholders, including parents, relatives, panchayat members, the police, NGOs, social workers should be sensitised and convinced about the negative impact of child marriage on children and about protecting the sexual and reproductive health and rights of girls.

Conclusion

We must understand that child marriage does not only constitute a single rights violation, but it also endangers the survival and well-being of women and girls by exposing them to sexual violence at an early stage, unplanned and frequent pregnancies, a denial of educational opportunities, and isolation from society. The National Commission for Protection of Child Rights (NCPCR) chairperson Shanta Sinha stressed the need for a public awareness campaign in favour of girl children. All stakeholders should be sensitised and convinced about the negative impacts of child marriage. Media can play a proactive role in creating awareness regarding child marriages at the district level.

REFERENCES

Bhat, A. Sen and U. Pradhan, 2005. "Child Marriage and the Law in India", *Human Rights Law Network*, New Delhi. p. 259.

Goswami, Sambodh, 2007. *Female Infanticide and Child Marriage*, Rawat Publication, Jaipur.

Jejeebhoy, Shireen, 1999. "Reproductive Health Information in India: What are the Gaps?", *Economic and Political Weekly*.

Sagade, Jaya, 2005. *Child Marriage in India: Socio-Legal and Human Rights*, Oxford University Press, New Delhi.

The Hindu, 2013, "Concern Over India's Refusal to Sign Child Marriage Resolution", 27th October.

The Hindustan Times, 2013. "India Ditches UN Resolution on Forced Child Marriage", October 16, Kolkata.

The Prohibition of Child Marriage Act 2006.

The Statesman, 2013. "Child Marriage Fairs a Hit in West Midnapore", October 22, Kolkata.

UNICEF 2005. Early Marriage: A Harmful Traditional Practice: A Statistical Exploration.

UNICEF, 2009. *State of the World's Children*.

UNICEF, 2010. *Progress for Children*.

Yadav, K.P., 2006. *Child Marriage in India*, Adhyayan Publishers & Distributors, New Delhi.

Websites

https://en.wikipedia.org/wiki/Child_marriage
www.csrindia.org
www.girlsnotbride.org
www.haqcrc.org
www.savegirlchild.org
www.unicef.org
www.wcd.nic.in/bsy.htm
www.wcd.nic.in/empowerment.htm
www.wcd.nic.in/ksy
www.wcd.nic.in/nationalcharter2003.htm

9

GIRL'S SUBJUGATION THROUGH HONOUR KILLINGS

Parents are the best protectors of their children. That is the order of human nature, but there have been freaks in the history of mankind. . . . They have extirpated (destroyed) their own daughter who hardly saw 14 summers of her life and the servant . . . in the breach of the commandment "thou shall not kill which God has created sacred".

Justice Shyam Lal in Aarushi Case (*The Telegraph*, 2013:1)

Introduction

An honour killing is the homicide of a member of a family or social group by other members, due to the belief of the perpetrators that the victim has brought dishonour or shame upon the family or community. Victims of honour killings are killed for reasons such as refusing to enter an arranged marriage, being in a relationship that is disapproved by their relatives, having sex outside marriage, becoming the victim of rape, dressing in ways which are deemed inappropriate. It is a cold blooded murder where parents of the girl seem to be against their daughter's affair. "Honour" crimes are common in Haryana, Punjab and Uttar Pradesh. There are no statistics on the number of "honour" killings across Haryana and Punjab, but according to a study, hundreds of people are killed each year for falling in love or marrying against their families' wishes.

Human Right Watch defines it as acts of vengeance, usually death, committed by male family members against female family members, who are held to have brought dishonour upon the family. A woman can be targeted by (individuals within) her family for a variety of reasons, including: refusing to enter into an arranged marriage, being the victim of a sexual assault, seeking a divorce — even from an abusive husband — or (allegedly) committing adultery. The mere perception that a woman has behaved in a way that "dishonours" her family is sufficient to trigger an attack on her life. An Amnesty International statement adds that the regime of honour is unforgiving: women on whom suspicion has fallen are not given an opportunity to defend themselves, and family members have no socially acceptable alternative but to remove the stain on their honour by attacking the woman.

The ideology of honour, being a gendered notion in India, both men and women embody notions of honour in totally different ways. Woman is the repository of the family honour as a daughter, wife and mother while man regulates it. The greatest threat to this honour lies in the woman, in her body, conduct due to her reproducing and procreating capacity (Chowdhary, 2007:16). Honour is presumed to be female linked commodity coupled with the male prerogative to ensure that she does not jeopardise its delicate balance at any cost. As a girl grows up, burden of shame accompanying her femaleness makes it difficult for her to be proud of her body (Nabar, 1995:87). Since she represents fertility and growth, separate from the male and not under his control, her power is seen as dangerous, malevolent and potentially a destructive force (Dewan, 2000:35).

A man's honour largely lies in his ability to impose such control on his womenfolk. All decisions regarding her body is made by the male members of her family and caste. The whole clan, caste and community are the co-sharers of this honour as blood ties of the family extend to them (Chowdhary, 2007:16). The social relationship of marriage subdues this dangerous force of the female. Male acting as a restraining factor becomes supreme by subordinating her in marriage (Dewan, 2000:35).

Being the repository of the family and caste honour, a woman is rendered an object of protection and violence at the same time. The fear of losing this honour makes the men rationalise and justify masculine aggression and violence against her. Violence against her within the four walls of the house in the capacity of a daughter, sister, wife and mother is widely accepted and legitimised under the patriarchal order and ultimately transcends caste divisions. Violence against her has a public face and is always committed in response to the cultural expectations of the larger community (Chowdhary, 2007:17). Even if the family wishes, it is not allowed to settle the matter of inter-caste marriages amicably, but is compelled to treat it as a matter of honour by the community which is ready to take over if the family is unwilling, thereby forcing the family to sacrifice their daughters in the collective interests of the caste group. The concept of honour operates at the cost of human sentiments and values.

HISTORICAL BACKGROUND OF HONOUR KILLING

The honour killing emerged in the pre-Islamic era but got strengthened in Islamic period. The honour killing stemmed from the patriarchal and patrilineal society's interest in maintaining strict control over designated familiar power structures. The honour of a family is very much depended on a woman's virginity. A woman's virginity is the property of the men around her, first her father, later a gift for her husband. The family is directly responsible of defending its honour.

Originally as per a Baluch and Pashtun custom, honour killings are founded in the twin concepts of honour and commodification of women. Women are married off for a bride price paid to the father. This was basically a Baluch and Pashtun tribal custom. Honour killings are not only reported in Baluchistan, NWFP and Upper Sindh which has a Baluch influx, but in Punjab provinces as well. If this commodity is damaged the proprietor, the father for alleged sexual misbehaviour and alleged 'lover' gets away, the latter has to pay the husband compensation for the wife that was lost and for his own wife, which was spared. Often the dead woman's alleged, 'lover' hands over a sister to the husband, in addition to a larger amount of money (Behera, 2013:50).

Genesis of Inter-Caste Marriage in India

In spite of strict caste endogamous rules in India, inter-caste marriages are a regular feature (Chowdhary, 2007:46). Inbreeding among different castes or *varnas* known as *sankarat sa eva varnam* (Roohi and Samaddar, 2009:509), *jati-sansakara* or *varna-sansakara* (Sharma, 2004:67) was a common feature in ancient India. This is evident from *Manusmriti* which deals elaborately with the rules relating to marriage among the mixed caste (Buhler, 1990:83) and *Yajnavalkyasmriti* dealing with shares of sons born from wives of different castes (Altekar, 1959:76). Manu allowed a woman to choose her own partner only if her parents failed to arrange her marriage within three years of her attaining puberty.

The rules of marriage within the caste were established in the post-Aryan period when caste become hereditary (Liddle and Joshi, 1986:61). Tough women enjoyed equal rights in selecting marital partner in the Vedic period (Dewan, 2000:33), the parents exercised great control in this regard. Festive gatherings called as *Samana* provided ample opportunity of love-making to the young men and women ending in marriage (Tripathy, 2000:32). Kshatriya brides enjoyed the right of selecting consorts in *svayamvaras* (Altekar, 195:65).

In the post-Vedic period, the rights and privileges of women came to be restricted. In the fifth century A.D. selection of partners by the girls without being authorised by their guardians was regarded as unmannerly (Altekar, 1959:69). After thc tenth century A.D., they came to be further disapproved due to the widening cultural differences between the *Brahmanas* and the other castes. Amidst conflicts and opposition, instances of inter-caste, inter-religious marriages have been on the rise in the post-colonial India due to Westernisation and woman empowerment. Though these marriages are constitutional, these exists no social acceptance for them (Tripathy, 2000:95).

FACTORS RESPONSIBLE FOR HONOUR KILLING

Indian women have been the victim of humiliation, torture, exploitation and face the risk of the worst violence, terror, deprivation, discrimination and devaluation. Some of the factors responsible for honour killing are —

Cultural Reason

Changing cultural and economic status of women has also been used to explain the occurrences of honour killings. Women in largely patriarchal cultures who have gained economic independence from their families go against their male-dominated culture. Some researchers argue that the shift towards greater responsibility for women and less for their fathers may cause their male family members to act in oppressive and sometimes violent manners in order to regain authority.

This change of culture can also be seen to have an effect in Western cultures such as Britain where honour killings often arise from women seeking greater independence and adopting seemingly Western values. For women who trace their ancestry back to the Middle East or South Asia, wearing clothes that are considered Western, having a boyfriend, or refusing to accept an arranged marriage are all offenses that can and have led to an honour killing.

People, who live in culture of honour, perceive family as the central institution in their society and a person's social identity depends largely on their family. Therefore, it is important for these individuals to fulfil expectations of family and society in order to be accepted by their family and experience feelings of belonging to this central institution that they are tied through birth or marriage. In some cultures, maintaining family honour is perceived as more important than either individual freedom, or individual achievement.

Social Factor

The reason for increasing in honour killing is the fear of losing their caste status through which they gain many benefits which makes them commit this heinous crime. The mentality of people has not changed and they cannot accept that marriage can take place in the same *gotra* or outside one's caste. The belief that persons from same *gotra* are siblings and should not marry has no rational basis. Yet marriage between persons from the same *gotra* seems to evoke a great deal of moral indignation, fury and rage enough to warrant brutal killing. The root of the cause for the increase in the number of honour killing is because formal governance has not been able to reach the rural areas and as a result this practice continues (Rana, 2013:40).

Whenever, a young couple elopes after marriage or for marrying, usually the girl's family tries to criminalise their action and contest the validity of the marriage. It is alleged that the girl is a minor and charges of kidnaping, abduction, wrongful confinement or rape is slapped against her husband and his family members for harassing them. For the loss of their family's honour, the honour of the offending family is attacked. This strategy is adopted to force the married couple to surface or to withdraw from the much disputed marriage. After surfacing, in majority of the cases, they run the risk of humiliation, physical injuries, death and decision of caste *panchayats*. Death penalty is regarded a valid method of retrieving the lost honour. At times, the woman is pressurised by her family to support their case of kidnaping or is sometimes solitarily confined by the family members or is sent to the state run protective homes (Welchman & Hossain, 2005:308).

Legal Awareness

Increasing legal awareness amongst women. More women are now aware of their rights. This credit legally goes not only to the awareness raising work by women's rights groups but also to the media and mobility of women. Women's refusal comply with the decision or traditions to violate their newly discovered rights has led to backlash from men apprehending loss of control, involving, violence, killing and other such threats.

The Role of *Khap* Panchayat

Khap panchayat or Caste council covers 84 villages. The *Khap panchayats* have unwritten law, and their decisions are clearly illegal and extra-constitutional. The *Khap panchayat* is a creation of the *Jats*. Each caste has a separate caste council and a leader for every *gotra* or lineage. Most of the *khap panchayat diktats* are against couples who are not from the same *gotra*. In fact, not more than one case of honour killing has been of a couple within the same *gotra*. By creating the false impression that all marriages of choice between young couples are incestuous, what the *khaps* are actually opposing is the right to choose a marriage partner. Among the several instances of *khaps* issuing *fatwas* in Jaundhi, Asanda, Dharana, Singhwal, Hadaudi, Maham-Kheri, Ludana and other villages, not a single one was an intra-*gotra* marriage, yet the married couples were declared siblings, and families made to suffer boycotts and excommunication from their villages (*The Hindu*, 2010).

A sad example of the *gotra* row is that of Ved Pal Moan, brutally beaten to death in 2009 when he tried to secure his wife who was confined by her parents at Singhwal village in Jind district. He was escorted by a police party and a warrant officer of the High Court. Ved Pal had married neither within his *gotra* nor within the same village. In this case, another absurd code was invoked by the *khap:* that the couple violated the custom of not marrying in the neighbouring village as it forms part of *bhaichara* (brotherhood). A *khap* congregation held in March 2009 publicly pronounced the death sentence for Ved Pal, and it succeeded in executing it in June. As couples are selectively targeted, it is clear the real motive is to control women's sexuality to ensure that property remains within the patriarchal caste domain (mainly Jats in Haryana). The restrictions imposed by *Khap panchayat* with respect to Jat marriages are —

- Marriage within the same *gotra* is forbidden since in that case a boy and girl are regarded as a brother and sister.
- Marriages in different *gotras* are forbidden if a boy and girl belong to the same village or physically adjoining villages.
- Inter-caste marriages are strictly taboo.

In a recent move Haryana's biggest *khap panchayat* called by Satrol *khap* in Hisar on 20th April, 2014 allowed inter-caste marriages as well as weddings between families from villages within the radius of 42 villages. Same *gotra* marriages, however, remain barred and the wedding can take place only with parental consent. Satrol panchayat cover 36 castes in 42 villages spread over 250 sq.km. area of Narnaund village of Hisar district and has 60 per cent population of Jats, who would be able to marry into different castes subject to parental approval. This will bring revolutionary change in Haryana (*The Times of India*, 2014:9).

Limited But Crucial Role of Judiciary

The judiciary does have a crucial role to play but has its limitations too. On June 23, 2008 Justice K.S. Ahluwalia of the Punjab and Haryana High Court made a revealing observation while simultaneously hearing 10 cases pertaining to marriages between young couples aged 18-21: "The High Court is flooded with petitions where . . . judges of this Court have to answer for the right of life and liberty to married couples. The State is a mute spectator. When shall the State awake from its slumber [and] for how long can Courts provide solace and balm by disposing of such cases?" A legislature with little political will and a pliant executive will have to be made responsive under pressure of a mass movement. Supreme Court Directive in 2011 affirmed that honour killings should be treated as the "rarest of rare crime and those perpetrating it should be sent to the gallows".

Desiring to marry the person a girl loves is not an offence even if she is below 18, the Punjab and Haryana High Court has ruled on October 15, 2013 in a clear message to people supporting killings in the name of honour. The Court told police to provide protection to couples, who has got married against the wishes of their parents, in its common order. The ruling came in responses to different petitions from couples, including minors, seeking police protection from their parents and relatives. Justice Mahesh Grover of the vacation bench observed a young girl in love has two courses available — to marry with the consent of her parents or to wait for attaining age of 18. "A father has no right to forcibly marry off his daughter, who is even below 18 years against her wishes. Neither he has right to kill her because she intends to marry out of her religion," said the Judge. "If a girl around 17 years of age runs away from her parents' house to save herself from the onslaught of her father and relatives and joins her lover or runs away with him, it is no offence either on the part of the girl or on the part of the boy with whom she ran away and married." The HC referred to various Supreme Court judgements and observed if parents do not agree to such alliances, the couple has a right to protect themselves (*The Times of India*, 2013:13).

Human Rights Perspective

The term the "girl child" describes a female child up to the age of eighteen. When referring to the girl child a clear distinction needs to be made between the terms sex and gender. Biological characteristics identify the sex of an individual as male or female. Gender, on the other hand, is a social construct. Gender is what it means in a particular society to be male or female. Gender attributes include codes of behaviour considered appropriate to each gender, along with a division of labour between two genders. The girl child quickly learns there is a high price to pay for being born a girl. Discrimination against the girl child is with her from the womb:

- ***Pre-birth :*** Ultrasound and amniocentesis test results are used to abort unwanted baby girls.
- ***Infancy :*** Female infants experience infanticide and discriminatory neglect; girls are also breastfed less and weaned earlier.
- ***Childhood :*** Girls receive less nourishing food, and are immunised less and taken for medical care later and in worse condition than boys; girls get much less education and have to work up to twice as many hours in the home as boys.
- ***Pre-adolescence :*** Girls are married off much earlier than boys.
- ***Adolescence :*** As child brides, many girls get pregnant in their teenage years, facing great health risks for themselves and their babies. (UNICEF, State of the World's Children, 2007).

A recent World Vision report stated why it is crucial to support girl child issues: "Girls are the world's most squandered gift. They are precious human beings with enormous potential, but across the world, they are generally the last to have their basic needs met and the first to have their basic rights denied" (*World Vision*, 2001).

It is pertinent to mention that a human rights approach perspective may be very useful in fight against honour killing. International human rights law offers an established and internationally recognised framework for obtaining redress violation of human rights. Victims of human killing are threatened by their families find neither understanding nor refuse in their communities and no redress before Judiciary. For them and for their families International Human Rights Law provides mechanism for challenging regimes that fail to protect the fundamental rights of their citizens (Moharana, 2013:28).

The Committee on the Elimination of Discrimination against Women (CEDAW) has emphasised that honour killing are a violation of the right to life and security of person. The Committee has urged governments to respect and promote the human rights of women over discriminatory cultural practices and to take "effective and proactive measures" to eliminate discrimination and violence against women in general and in immigrant and minority communities. In addition to enacting laws criminalising harmful cultural practice, such measures should include awareness — raising programme, programme to sensitise the community to combat patriarchal attitudes, practices and stereotype role. The CEDAW committee has expressed its concerned that women of ethnic and minority communities have limited information concerning their rights, including their right to be free from violence such as honour killing. The CEDAW committee has also called for a holistic approach to prevention and elimination of violence against women, including honour killing.

The Committee monitoring the Convention of the Right of the Child (CRC), has expressed deep concern about the violence of the right to life that occur in the form of honour killings. The CRC has emphasised that honour killing violate Article 2 (non-discrimination), Article 3 (best interest of the child), Article 6 (right to life), Article 19 (protection from all forms of violence). It has recommended the Government to develop and effectively implement an awareness and education campaign to combat effectively discriminatory attitudes and harmful traditions affecting girls. Such a campaign should involve religious and community leaders.

Suggestions

The usual remedies against to fight such social onslaught is to require immediate sensitisation; police officials/law enforcement agencies, setting up women police station in the *Khap* belt, counselling women victims and civil administration:

- The Special Marriage Act 1954 needs to be amended for the removal of 30 days waiting period for registering a marriage provided there is a mutual consent and both are above the legally permissible age.
- Special clause should be added to Section 300 of the Indian Penal Code to deal with the cases like houour killing.
- It gives a wrong message that *Khap Panchayat* has their own law and they adjudicate not according to laid down any

procedure but summarily which they deem fit. They have scant regards to judicial institutions and courts. The steps be taken whosoever is involved in the crime and how so great he may be should immediately be brought under the law (Rana, 2013:46).

- The real remedy for breaking caste is inter-caste marriage. Nothing else will serve as a solvent of caste (Dr. B. R. Ambedkar).
- The power of the caste panchayats need to be curtailed by appropriate legislation.
- The common man and the general public ought to be enlightened about the importance of the female population, the value of life and the horrors of the honour killing through massive and large scale campaigns, public debates and discussion, media coverage and so on. The family and the community attitude towards these crimes can be combated and checked only by having a discourse with them and no strategy in this direction will be successful without their consent and cooperation.
- A wider social movement needs to be launched for making the women aware of their legal rights and in making them understand and accept that there exists no violation of the family honour or caste honour, if she educates herself, develops her personality, express her desire in making marital choice, develops friendships with opposite sex and chooses to work.

Conclusion

Prohibition of inter-religious, intra-*gotra* marriages, inter- and intra-regional marriages are an indication of forcible imposition of the male dominated hierarchical marriages. The patriarchy is rigidly segmenting the whole mankind into various mutually rival groups. The concepts of 'honour' and 'shame' operate to restore the male dominance which is presumed to have been compromised and endangered by the post-colonial legal empowerment of woman in India. Honour killing is a shame on the face of civil society. The level of cruelty displayed in this shameful crime has stirred the conscience of all right thinking individuals. Honour killing is a barbaric crime continues unabated and reminding of medieval period. Haryana alone has recorded dozens of honour killing incidents, but nothing has been done to curb such crimes against humanity. It is ironical that the State Government and mainstream politics continue to be silent spectators due to which no strong signal goes to the perpetrators of such crimes. The All India Democratic Women's Association (AIDWA) had long been striving for enactment of a separate legislation against honour killings, in this regard "a memorandum, with over a lakh signatures, was submitted to the Union Law Minister a few months back and draft legislation too was submitted to the Ministry." But the same was not placed before Parliament owing to opposition by Haryana Government and other regressive forces like *Khaps* who are active in the north-western region. AIDWA also exhorted the elders to ponder over the concept of family honour and raise questions as to what honour was being saved by killing our own children. Honour killings should be dealt with heavy penalty. The mind set of the people need to change. Parents and village elders should accept the children's wishes and sentiments regarding marriage as it is they who will lead a life with their life partner.

REFERENCES

Ahlawat, Neerja, 2012. "The Political Economy of Haryana's *Khap*", *Economic and Political Weekly*, Vol. XLVII, No. 47-48, pp. 15-17.

Alston, Philips, 1984. "Conjuring Up New Human Rights: A Proposal for Quality Control", *The American Journal of International Law*, Vol. 78, No. 3, 607-21.

Altekar, A.S., 1959. *The Position of Women in Hindu Civilization: From Prehistoric Times to the Present Day*, Motilal Banarsidass Publishers, Delhi.

Annavararpu, Sneha, 2013. "Human Rights, Honour Killing and the Indian Law", *Economic and Political Weekly*, December 14, Vol. XLVIII, No. 50, pp. 129-32.

Behera, Avimanyu, 2013. "Honour Killing", *Indian Bar Review*, Vol. XL(1), pp. 47-62.

Chesler, Phyllis, 2010. "Worldwide Trends in Honour Killing", *Middle East Quarterly*, Spring, 3-11.

Chowdhary, P., 2007. *Contentious Marriage, Eloping Couples: Gender, Caste and Patriarchy in Northern India*, Oxford University Press, New Delhi.

Dash, Madhu Sudhan, 2012. "Rational of Honour Killing", *Indian Bar Review*, Vol. XXXIX(3), pp. 145-51.

Dewan, V.K., 2000. *Law Relating to Offences Against Women*, Orient Law House, New Delhi.

GoI, 2008. *Laws of Civil Marriages in India — A Proposal to Resolve Certain Conflicts* (Report No. 212) (New Delhi: Law Commission of India, Government of India).

GoI, 2012. *Prevention of Interference with the Freedom of Matrimonial Alliances (in the Name of Honour and Tradition): A Suggested Legal Framework* (New Delhi: Law Commission of India, Government of India).

Kachhwaha, Kavita, 2011. "*Khap* Adjudication in India: Honouring The Culture with Crimes", *International Journal of Criminal Justice Science*, Vol. 6, Issue 1-2: 297-308.

Moharana, S.D., 2013. "Honour Killing on the International Humanitarian Law", *Indian Bar Review*, Vol. XL(1), pp. 25-36.

Nabar, V., 1995. *Caste as Woman*, Penguin Books, New Delhi.

Rana, Pranab Kumar, 2013. "Socio-Legal Perspective on Honour Killing in India: A Case for False Projection of Patriarchy", *Indian Bar Review*, Vol. XL(1), pp. 37-46.

Roohi, S. and Samaddar, R., 2009. *Key Texts on Social Justice in India*, Sage Publication, New Delhi.

Sharma, A., 2004. *Hinduism and Human Rights: A Conceptual Approach*, Oxford University Press, New Delhi.

The Hindu, 2010. "*Khap* Panchayat: Signs of Desperation?", May 7.

The Statesman, 2013. "Honour Killing: HC Wamts Girl's Statement", November 19, Kolkata, p. 2.

The Telegraph, 2013. "Aarushi Parents Held Guilty", November 26, Kolkata, p. 1.

The Times of India, 2013. "Ok if Monors Elope to Wed", October 19, Kolkata, p. 13.

The Times of India, 2014. "Haryana *Khap* Allows Inter-Caste Weddings", April 21, Kolkata, p. 9.

Tripathy, P.C., 2000. *Crime Against Women*, APH Publishing Corp., New Delhi.

Welchman, L. and Hossain, S. (Ed.), 2005. *Honour*, Zed Books, London.

Yadav, Bhupendra, 2009. "*Khap Panchayats:* Stealing Freedom?", *Economic and Political Weekly*, December 26, Vol. XLIV, No. 52, pp. 16-19.

Websites

www.unicef.org
www.worldvision.org

10

CHILD RAPE

The Supreme Court of India has pronounced on October 26, 2015 that "Those who sexually assaulted minors were nothing but animals and deserved no leniency".

The Times of India, 2015 : 1

Introduction

Rape is a type of sexual assault usually involving sexual intercourse, which is initiated by one or more persons against another person without that person's consent. The act may be carried out by physical force, coercion, abuse of authority or against a person who is incapable of valid consent, such as one who is unconscious, incapacitated, or below the legal age of consent. The sexual use, involving penile, digital (fingers) or objects on a woman's or child's body without that person's consent, with forced consent (threats) or if that person cannot consent due to age, mental disability, state of drunkeness or druggedness, or relative social position to the rapist (employee, slave, patient, lower rank, parishioner, etc.). It can include penis in vagina, anus, or mouth, or forced masturbation. It can include objects. It can include rubbing genitals on a person with clothes in between. Women can, but rarely do, rape people by forcing them to touch or otherwise sexually interact. People of any age can be raped.

FACTORS CONTRIBUTE TO INCREASE RAPE

Poverty

Poor girls may be more at risk of rape in the course of their daily tasks than those who are better off, for example when they walk home on their own from work late at night, or work in the fields or collect firewood alone. Children of poor women may have less parental supervision when not in school, since their mothers may be at work and unable to afford child care. The children themselves may, in fact, be working and thus vulnerable to sexual exploitation. Poverty forces many girls into occupations that carry a relatively high risk of sexual violence, particularly sex work. It also creates enormous pressures for them to find or maintain jobs, to pursue trading activities and, if studying, to obtain good grades, all of which render them vulnerable to sexual coercion from those who can promise these things.

Aggravating Factors

An offence of rape will be considered grave when one or more of aggravating factors are present. The offence of rape consists of aggravating factors when it is committed by two or more offenders; when the offender is in a position of trust or confidence of the victim; there is an element of abduction along with the offence of rape. Rape of a child or other vulnerable victim; rape aggravated by discrimination; repeated penetration in the course of a single attack; and rape by an offender with a life threatening sexually transmitted diseases.

Aggravating factors also include matters such as:

- the careful planning of the rape;
- breaking into a house to commit rape knowing the presence of the victim alone inside the house;
- covert use of a drug to overcome resistance or obliterate memory;
- the presence of children when the rape is committed; and
- a history of sexual assaults or violence by the offender against the victim.

The Influence of Pornography

The number of victims of childhood sexual abuse and molestation grows each year. This horrific crime is directly tied to the growth of pornography on the Internet. Studies conducted by the various organisations have shown that pornography is extremely influential in the actions of sex offenders and serial murders. Further, statistics show that 90 per cent of the predators who molest children have had some type of involvement with pornography. According to research reveals that 77 per cent of child molesters of boys and 87 per cent of child molesters of girls admitted imitating the sexual behaviour they had seen in pornography they had watched. Roughly 33 per cent of girls and 14 per cent of boys are molested before the age of 18, according to various state departments. Nearly 2/3 of all sexual assaults reported involved minors and roughly 1/3 involved children under the age of 12. In most cases, however, child molestation goes unreported. Estimates are that only a small percentage although some say that only 35 per cent of sexual abuse is reported. Kids can be frightened or embarrassed and many times do not say anything.

Computer Predators

Since, many children today spend time on the electronic super highway "surfing the net," it is not surprising that child molesters go there to look for victims. "Chat rooms," have become the "playgrounds" of the 90s. A molester engages a child in a chat-room by posing on-line as a child himself. Once an on-line relationship is established the molester will often suggest a conversation in a "private room", i.e. a chat room for only two. Then language becomes sexually explicit, pornography can be transmitted electronically, and the relationship becomes abusive.

CRIME AGAINST CHILDREN

The offences committed against children or the crimes in which children are the victims are considered as crime against children. Indian Penal Code (IPC) and the various protective and preventive special and local laws specifically mention the offences wherein children are victims. An offence committed on a victim under the age of 18 years is constructed as crime against children.

Table 10.1 shows that a total of 38,172 cases of crimes against children were reported in the country during 2012 as compared to 33,098 cases during 2011, suggesting an increase of 15.3 per cent. Among IPC crimes, a total of 1,678 cases of murder of children (including infanticide) were reported in the country against 1,514 cases in 2011 resulting in an increase of 10.8 per cent in 2012 over 2011. A total of 8,541 cases of child rape were reported in the country during 2012 as compared to 7,112 in 2011 accounting for an increase of 20.1 per cent during the year 2012. According to Crime Record Bureau Madhya Pradesh has reported the highest number of cases (1632) followed by Uttar Pradesh (1040) and Maharashtra (917).These three States together accounted for 42 per cent of the total child rape cases reported in the country. A total of 18,266 cases of kidnapping and abduction of children were reported during the year 2012 as compared to 15,284 cases in the previous year accounting for a increase of 19.5 per cent. In case of abetment to suicide, total 144 cases of abetment to suicide by children were reported during the year 2012 as compared to 61 cases in the year 2011 denoting an increase of 136.1 per cent during the year 2012. Number of cases under procuration of minor girls decreased from 862 in 2011 to 809 in 2012, registering a decrease of 6.1 per cent over 2011. The cases of kidnapping and abduction have increased by 19.5 per cent during the year (from 15,284 in 2011 to 18,266 in 2012). Total 15 cases of Buying of Girls and 108 cases of Selling of Girls for prostitution were reported in the country during the year 2012 against 27 and 113 such cases respectively in the year 2011. Thus, it can be said that crime against children especially rape has increased in 2012 in comparison to 2011.

Table 10.1: Crime against Children in the Country and Percentage Variation in 2012 over 2011

Sl.No.	*Crime Head*	*Year*			*% Variation in*
		2010	*2011*	*2012*	*2012 over 2011*
1.	Murder	1,408	1,451	1,597	10.1
2.	Infanticide	100	63	81	28.6
3.	Rape	5,484	7,112	8,541	20.1
4.	Kidnapping and Abduction	10,670	15,284	18,266	19.5
5.	Foeticide	111	132	210	59.1
6.	Abetment or suicide	56	61	144	136.1
7.	Exposure and abandonment	725	700	821	17.3
8.	Procuration of minor girls	679	862	809	–6.1
9.	Buying of girls for prostitution	78	27	15	–44.1
10.	Selling of girls for prostitution	130	113	108	–4.4
11.	Others crimes (including Prohibition of Child Marriage Act, 2006)	7,253	7,293	7,580	3.9
	Total	**26,694**	**33,098**	**38,172**	**15.3**

Source: Crime Record Bureau Report 2012.

According to National Crime Record Bureau Report 2014, a total of 13,766 cases of child rape were reported in the country during 2014 as compared to 12,363 in 2013 accounting for an increase of 11.3 per cent during the year 2014. Maximum numbers of child rape cases were reported in Madhya Pradesh (2,352 cases) followed by Maharashtra (1,714) and Uttar Pradesh (1,538 cases). Total number of victims was 13,833 in 13,766 cases.

CASE STUDY OF RAPE VICTIMS

Madhyamgram Victim

The Madhyamgram gang rape victim's father filed a plea in Calcutta High Court on 6th January, 2014, seeking a CBI probe into the series of events that led to the ghastly death of his teenage daughter. He felt the state has failed to conduct free and fair investigation. Victim's father narrated that his daughter came from Bihar to study. A couple of years ago, she passed her class VI examination from Saket Bihari Sanskrit Vidyalaya in Bihar. She went missing on the night of October 25, 2013, only to return the next day, scared and traumatised. That night she told her parents that she was gang-raped in an open field. When the victim and her father went to lodge a complaint, he was made to wait for nine hours before the FIR was registered. The next day, his daughter was raped again.

He alleges when he went to lodge the second complaint, police forcibly made him sign and acknowledge a written complaint with distorted facts. That she was raped again was not borne out by the second FIR. He claims it was filed against one 'Chhottu' and no one else. Traumatised and scared he says, he chose to shift to a new home off the airport on November 13, 2013. This was traced by the confidants of the accused. They kept up their threats and taking advantage of his absence and also that of his wife — they set the victim on fire on November 23, 2013. Admitted to RG Kar Hospital the same day, his daughter was denied minimum treatment and the hospital scoffed at their repeated pleas to transfer her to SSKM burn ward.

Victim father also argues that right to life, which is a fundamental right, was not ensured here as police failed to protect a rape victim and her tormented family. Instead, he alleges that police were desperate to cremate the body before daybreak on January 1, 2014 and that they even hijacked the hearse and continuously threatened them at their home. He was asked to go back to Bihar and a policeman even threatened to stop him from plying his taxi. His father argues that the state and police had purposefully neglected giving the victim any respite, for she was poor and from Bihar.

Park Street Victim

A 13-years old girl is a pavement dweller on Park Street and was on her way to a night shelter run by an NGO for children when she was abducted on the lure of a hot meal. Her mother had been sending her to the shelter for the past few days to save her from the biting cold.

"On December 22, 2013 evening, the child set off for the shelter, a short walk away, but decided to drop in at the house of a friend on Collin Lane for a short while. She left as soon as her friend's husband returned around 11 p.m. She was walking to the shelter when 32-years old Md. Anwar stopped her near a restaurant on Rafi Ahmed Kidwai Road," say police. He gave her a meal and asked her to wait for more Christmas goodies.

According to police source, the accused hailed a cab that already had an occupant besides the driver. As the taxi began moving towards Tricona Park on Ripon Street, the accused took turns to rape her inside the taxi. Even the taxi driver joined in the sexual assault, says the girl. The child is too traumatised to remember the road she was drove through. She was driven through. She was dumped back on Rafi Ahmed Kidwai Road around 4 a.m.

Delhi School Girl Victim

A 16-year old school girl from South Delhi was raped by three friends on October 22, 2013. The class 10 student told the police the three friends picked her up at 7.30 p.m. for an outing in the Safdarjung area and gave her an alcohol-spiked beverage. "She was picked up by two of the men in a white Hondai Verna car and offered a ride. She decided to go along them since she knew them," said a police officer. They were soon joined by the third accused and they drove to the parking lot of nearby Kamal Cinema, where they raped her and threatened her against telling anyone. The three men dropped her at a fair distance from her home and are on the run. A complaint was filed at Safdarjung Enclave police station by the victim's father after he saw her stumbling, apparently drunken, around 1 a.m. Her father asked her what the matter and she broke down and told him what had happened. A medical examination confirmed sexual assault and a case of gang rape has been registered.

Gaighata Case

A gang of three allegedly gang-raped a 15 years old girl and filmed the sexual assault on mobile phones in Gaighata on January 10, 2014 evening. They threatened to make the video public if she dared to tell anyone about it, but the victim went to police and filed a complaint, naming them and a woman who had lured her to the trio.

According to the girl's complaint, she was returning home after buying some textbooks at 8.30 pm on Friday when a woman stopped her. On the way she met Shukla Mondal, who gave her false information and took her to a field where the three youths were waiting. She tried to escape, but they dragged her away to a corner of the field, raped her and took pictures on their mobiles. The Police have arrested the three accused named in the FIR and placed a police picket at the victim's home.

LEGAL FRAMEWORK IN INDIA

On May 22, 2012, Parliament passed the Protection of Children from Sexual Offences Act, 2012 (POCSO), which came into force on November 14, 2012, this special law to protect children from offences of sexual assault, sexual harassment and pornography, remains an unimplemented law, unknown to most and beyond the reach of those who need to apply it. Sadly, the result is that POCSO — a necessity in India where 40 per cent of the population is below the age of 18 and where over 53 per cent of children reportedly surveyed in 2007 stated that they had experienced one or more forms of sexual abuse — is not complied with despite being in the statute book. There are demands for stiff penalties, expeditious new laws and fast-track courts although POCSO, as a wholesome law, already says it all.

The enactment of POCSO Act is one such genuine attempt by the legislators to create the desired enabling environment by empowering the children and strengthening the legal provisions for their protection from sexual abuse and exploitation. The Act purports to protect persons below the age of 18 years from offences such as sexual assault, sexual harassment and child pornography, all of which have been accurately defined and are accompanied by rigorous punishment proportionate to the gravity of the crime.

In fact, the wisdom of the legislators is well brought forth in Sections 5 and 9 of the Act which overtly classifies and penalises the act of penetrative sexual assault and sexual assault by a police officer, member of armed forces, public servant, being on the management or on the staff of a jail or remand home as aggravated penetrative sexual assault and aggravated sexual assault respectively to severely reprimand the person who commit such offences despite their high status and responsible post. These provisions send out a strong message in general, which will aid in wider curbing of such offences by public servants and by persons in responsible posts.

Salient Features of The POCSO Act

Before this Act, various provisions of the Indian Penal Code (IPC) were used to deal with sexual offences against children as the law did not make a distinction between an adult and a child. POCSO deals with sexual offences against persons below 18, who are deemed as children. POCSO provides definitions of "penetrative sexual assault", "sexual assault" and "sexual harassment".

- This is the first time that an Act has listed aspects of touch as well as non-touch behaviour (photographing a child in a obscene manner) under the ambit of sexual offences.
- The Act incorporates child friendly procedures for reporting, recording of evidence, investigation and trial of offence.
- The attempt of commit an offence under the Act has also been made liable for punishment for up to half punishment prescribed for the commission of the offences.
- The Act also provides for punishment for abetment of the offence, which is the same as for the commission of the offence. This would cover trafficking of children for sexual purposes.
- For the more heinous offences of Penetrative Sexual Assault, Aggravated Penetrative Sexual Assault, Sexual Assault and Aggravated Sexual Assault, the burden of proof is shifted on the accused.
- The Act prescribed that the evidence of the child shall be recorded within a period of 30 days of the Special Court taking cognisance of the offence and reason for delay, if any, shall be recorded by the Special Court.
- The media has been barred from disclosing the identity of the child without the permission of the Special Court.

Unfortunately, trial and conviction of the rape accused is painfully slow; even the Supreme Court deplored the delay and conviction rate. Many cases are negligently investigated by the police, particularly when the rape victims are from poor families, which is very often the case. The victim's ordeal in the court of law is worse (*The Statesman*, 2013:6). The Institute of Social Science had conducted a survey of the acquittal rape cases in Delhi courts, its finding mentioned that the victims invariably alleged that the prosecutors were callous and seldom consulted the affected girls and women before arguing their cases. Repeated adjournment of cases frustrated the victims. Legal experts say that the process of delay usually begins when the police take up a case. As rape cases rarely have eyewitnesses, collection of forensic evidence becomes crucial to cracking the case. But the police do not have proper training in investigation and collecting evidence.

The Mamta Banerjee Government in West Bengal has standardised an operative protocol for forensic medical examination of rape survivors, following a Supreme Court order in September 2013 (*The Times of India*, 2013:4). The salient features of the proforma are —

- Police or court cannot compel a victim to show her private parts for examination to a doctor.
- Lady attendants or nurse to aid the victim during the medical test if a lady doctor is not available.
- Doctors should give priority to treating the victim, rather than collecting sample or vaginal swab from the victim.
- Free counselling to be provided to the victim for her recovery, so that, she can get rid of long-term psychological problems
- Age estimation of the victim is to be done by proper medico-legal process.
- Legal support should be given to the rape victims.
- Information of rape to be given to the police quickly, so that, medical test can be done immediately.
- Specifications on collection of evidence (labelling bags, etc.).
- Assessment must be done for external evidence of trauma (abrasion, bruises, stab wounds, etc.).
- Saliva swab is to be preserved for DNA profile determination and comparison with that of the salivery swab of the assailant.
- Patient should be advised to be accompanied by the family members or relatives while leaving for the health care facility.

Factors That Delay Justice

- Sloppy investigation by police.
- Probes are mostly conducted by sub-inspectors with untrained constable.
- Eyewitnesses are rare and police are not properly trained to handle forensic evidence.
- There are only four central forensic laboratories and reports take too much time.
- Police witnesses not easily available, get transferred frequently.
- Defence lawyer seeks adjournment on frivolous grounds and judges often oblige them.

- Public prosecutors often cannot match the talent and commitment of defence lawyers.
- Judges are overburdened and can't give priority to rape cases.

In fact, India needs many more courts and judges to specifically deal with offences against women and child for quicker trial. Now, there are only 14 judges for one million people despite the Law Commission's recommen-dations and Supreme Court's directions that the number be raised to 50 (*The Hindustan Times*, 2013:9).

PSYCHOLOGICAL EFFECTS

Child sexual abuse can result in both short-term and long-term harm, including psychopathology in later life. Indicators and effects include depression, anxiety, eating disorders, poor self-esteem, somatisation, sleep disturbances, and anxiety disorders including post-traumatic stress disorder. While children may exhibit regressive behaviours such as a return to thumb-sucking or bed-wetting, the strongest indicator of sexual abuse is sexual acting out and inappropriate sexual knowledge and interest. Victims may withdraw from school and social activities exhibit various learning and behavioural problems including cruelty to animals, attention deficit/hyperactivity disorder (ADHD), conduct disorder, and oppositional defiant disorder (ODD). Teenage pregnancy and risky sexual behaviours may appear in adolescence. Child sexual abuse victims report almost four times as many incidences of self-inflicted harm.

DEBATE ON JUVENILE JUSTICE ACT 2000

Juvenile Justice (Care and Protection of Children) Act 2000 has been enacted with a view to provide proper care, protection and treatment of the children for their development and to provide child friendly approach in the matter of adjudication in the best interest of children. In order to achieve the said objective many beneficial provisions have also been incorporated in the Act. Bail to juvenile is the rule and denial is an exception. The juvenile shall not be sent to jail. He must be sent to either observation home or special home. But in no case the juvenile shall not be sent to a special home for a period of more than three years.

But the question remains if the juvenile is involved in the commission of heinous crime like murder or rape or commits the offences of rape and murder in order to satisfy his lust or take the revenge, can it be proper not to impose adequate punishment to the said wrongdoer/offender only on the ground that at the time of commission of the offence he was/

is a minor? True, the children should be dealt with a soft way. Another opportunity should be given to the children to reform and rectify him. It is true an honest and happy child is an asset to the country whereas a bitter and a broken child is a liability. Can the criminal attitude, if any inbred in the mind of the offender be removed by mere counselling? Group counselling and community service cannot change the attitude of the main perpetrator of crime. It is high time to evaluate or review the applicability or working of the Juvenile Justice (Care and Protection of Children) Act 2000.

The Union Cabinet has cleared Juvenile Justice (Care and Protection of Children) Bill 2014 on 22nd April, 2015 and it will place in Parliament very soon. The Bill states that in case a heinous crime has been committed by a person in the age group of 16-18 tears, it will be examined by a Juvenile Justice Board to assess if the crime was committed as a 'Child' or as an 'adult'. The trial of the case will take place accordingly by the board which will consist of psychologist and social expert. The legislation which would replace the existing Juvenile Justice Act 2000, was proposed in view of increasing number of serious offences being committed by person in the age group of 16-18 years (*The Statesman*, 2015:5).

According to data from the National Crime Record Bureau Report 2013, crimes by juveniles in the age group of 16-18 years have increased, especially in certain categories of heinous crime. The number of murder cases against juveniles rose from 531 in 2002 to 1007 in 2013. Similarly, cases of rape and assault with intent to outrage the modesty of women have gone up from 485 and 522 in 2002 to 1884 and 1424 in 2013 respectively. In 2013, 933 cases of kidnapping and abduction were registered against juveniles which were 704 in 2012.

Conclusion

Thus, rape is abominable and ghastly, and it worsens and becomes inhuman and barbaric when the victim, who is in a persistent vegetative state besides being a child, is subjected to unwanted physical contact by perverted male. The long-term solution for reducing crimes against girls is removal of societal and institutional prejudices against girls and gender sensitisation of society. Indian society is steeped in a patriarchal culture and has not yet learnt to respect girls and women. The prime need in child rape cases are to speed up the process of trial and imposed deterrent punishment like death sentence to perpetrators of grave offences. Rape victims should be encouraged to report cases to the police instead of cursing their lot with silent tears. Civil society and women's groups must conduct a vigorous campaign for social rehabilitation of rape victims and help them to come forward to expose the miscreants. Control of crime and improvement of law and order depends on the quality of policing, sensitivity of the officers and the rapport between the police and the public. Public prosecutors should understand the importance and sensitivity of rape cases and take action accordingly to ensure that judgment does not delayed.

REFERENCES

Advani, Poornima; Lina Gonslaves and J.K. Mittal, 2006. *Rape — A Legal Study*, New Delhi: National Commission for Women, p. 29.

GoI, 2012. "Protection of Children from Sexual Offences Act".

GoI, 2013. "The Criminal Law (Amendment) Act".

Julia, R. and Herman Schewendinger, 1993. *Rape and Inequality*, Sage Publications, California, 1993, p. 95.

National Crime Record Bureau Report, 2012.

National Crime Record Bureau Report, 2014.

Sathasivam, P., 2014. "Protection of Children from Sexual Offences Act 2012", *All India Reporter*, January, Vol. 101, Part 1201, p. 1.

The Hindustan Times, 2013. "16-Year Old Delhi School Girl Raped by Friends", October 25,.p. 10.

The Hindustan Times, 2013. "Justice Still a Far Cry all Three Rape Victims of Bengal even After 18 Months", September 13, p. 7.

The Hindustan Times, 2013. "Victim of Trial After Rape?", September 13, p. 9.

The Statesman, 2013. "Gangrape Again", September 7, Kolkata, p. 6.

The Statesman, 2013. "Minor Girls Sexually Assaulted", November 11, Kolkata, p. 13.

The Statesman, 2013. "Youth Gets Death for Rape", November 23, Kolkata, p. 3.

The Statesman, 2015. "Juvenile Justice Bill Likely this Week in Lok Sabha", May 4, Kolkata, p. 5.

The Times of India, 2013. "Child Kidnapped Near Park Street, Gang Raped", December 24, Kolkata, p. 1.

The Times of India, 2013. "Government Lays Down Rape Test Rules", November 6, Kolkata, p. 4.

The Times of India, 2013. "Rapist Jailed for the Rest of his Life", September 11, Kolkata, p. 7.

The Times of India, 2014. "CBI Probe Plea in Gang-rape Case", January 7, Kolkata, p. 4.

The Times of India, 2014. "Child Rapists are Like Animals, say SC", October 26, Kolkata, p. 1.

The Times of India, 2014. "Cops Offered Protection to Gariahata Rape Survivor", January 13, Kolkata, p. 3.

Sunday Times of India, 2014. "Trio Rape 15-Year Old, Films It on Mobile", January 3, Kolkata, p. 4.

Website

https://en.Wikipedia.org/Wiki/Rape

11

CHALLENGES OF ACID ATTACK ON GIRLS

Introduction

Acid throwing, also called an acid attack or vitriolage, is a form of violent assault. It is defined as the premeditated act of throwing acid on the body of a person "with the intention to disfigure, maim, torture, or kill". Perpetrators of these attacks throw acid at their victims, usually at their faces, burning them, and damaging skin tissue, often exposing and sometimes dissolving the bones. The victims of acid violence are overwhelmingly children and women and the perpetrators of the attacks are almost invariably young men, whose amorous or sexual advances have been spurned and who choose to "punish" the woman or girl in the cruelest manner. The attackers are familiar with the nature, habits and movement of girls and women on whom they intend to seek revenge and are, therefore, able to plan the attack in advance. The act rarely kills but causes severe physical, psychological and social scarring. The most common types of acid used in these attacks are sulphuric, nitric, or hydrochloric acid. The long-term consequences of these attacks include blindness and permanent scarring of the face and body, along with far-reaching economic difficulties. Acid violence is a world-wide phenomenon that is not restricted to a particular race, religion or geographical location. It is estimated there may be as many as 1,000 acid attacks a year in India, incidents that can kill, maim and wreck the lives of the victims (*The Hindustan Times*, 2013:1).

The data released by Home Ministry of India show that while a total of 57 cases with 65 victims were recorded in 2010, in 2012 the figure jumped to 85 cases with 101 victims. Delhi, Uttar Pradesh, Punjab, Haryana and Bihar together accounted for 53 per cent of all victims. In fact, Delhi (31 victims) along accounted for 27 per cent of all victims (264) in the country between 2010 and 2012. Police action has had little effect in curbing the crime is evident from the fact that in 225 cases in the given period, 318 people were arrested and 305 prosecuted (*Sunday Times of India*, 2014:7). Still, attacks kept increasing year by year. This data reveals that patriarchal societies like U.P., Delhi, Punjab, Haryana and Bihar who are having worst sex ratios — accounting for the most number of victims. Arrests and prosecution have had no deterring effect on the crime which kept on rising, making it a more problem of social attitude than a law and order issue. States in the north-east, where several societies are matriarchal and women make up a large chunk of the workforce, have nil to single digit cases of acid attacks. Among larger States, Tamil Nadu has one of the best records with just one case in the past three years.

The most notable effects of an acid attack are the lifelong bodily disfigurement. According to the Acid Survivors Foundation in Pakistan, there is a high survival rate amongst victims of acid attacks. Consequently, the victim is faced with physical challenges, which require long-term surgical treatment, as well as psychological challenges, which require in-depth intervention from psychologists and counsellors at each stage of physical recovery. These far-reaching effects on their lives impact their psychological, social and economic viability in communities.

Health Effect

The medical effects of acid attacks are extensive. Severity of the damage depends on the concentration of the acid and the period of time before the acid is thoroughly washed off with water or neutralised with a neutralising agent. The acid can rapidly eat away skin, the layer of fat beneath the skin, and in some cases even the underlying bone. Eyelids and lips may be completely destroyed, the nose and ears severely damaged. Though not exhaustive, their findings included: The skull is partly destroyed/deformed and hair lost. Some of other affects are —

- Ear cartilage is usually partly or totally destroyed; deafness may occur.
- Eyelids may be burned off or deformed, leaving the eyes extremely dry and prone to blindness. Acid directly in the eye also damages eye-sight, sometimes causing blindness in both eyes.
- Nose can become shrunken and deformed; the nostrils may close off completely due to destroyed cartilage.
- The mouth becomes shrunken and narrow, and it may lose its full range of motion. Sometimes, the lips may be partly or totally destroyed, exposing the teeth. Eating can become difficult.

- Scars can run down from the chin to neck area, shrinking the chin and extremely limiting range of motion in the neck.
- Inhalation of acid vapours usually create respiratory problems, exacerbated restricted airway pathways (the esophagus and nostrils) in acid patients.

In addition to these above-mentioned medical effects, acid attack victims also face the possibility of septicemia, renal failure, skin depigmentation, and even death. Skin should be grafted onto burn victims within a day or two to prevent infection.

Psychological Effect

Acid attacks are brutal, agonising and embarrassing to victims. Because of the disfigurement caused by acid, the victim's psyches are debilitated, incapacitated, negatively affecting every aspect of their lives (Anway, 2003:306).

Acid attack victims reported higher levels of anxiety, depression and scored higher on the Derriford appearance scale, which measures psychological distress due to one's concern for their appearance. Women suffered lowered self-esteem according to the Rosenberg scale and increased self-consciousness, both in general and in the social sphere. Shock, anger, self-pity and acceptance are the emotions that surface in the aftermath of an acid attack. These feelings are normal and must be accepted. Avoid blame games, families need to be supportive and let the victims grieve. Time and patience are crucial. People who learn to channelise their anger heal faster than those who got caught up in self-pity.

Victims have to undergo reconstructive surgeries. The prominent effect of an acid attack is lifelong bodily disfigurement. Consequently, the victim faces physical challenges, which require long-term surgical treatment, and psychological challenges, which require in-depth intervention from psychologists and counsellors at each stage of physical recovery.

Social Effect

Contact with acid can result in a wide range of injuries and even long-term or permanent damage depending on the concentration and volume used. It can cause burns, scars, dissolving of the skin and tissues underneath and even have a corrosive effect on the bones. Many survivors have to undergo a number of surgeries and other procedures on their eyes, nose, ears and skin on the face, neck and other parts of the body.

Acid attacks usually leave victims of handicapped in some way, rendering them dependent on either their spouse or family for everyday activities, such as eating and running errands. This dependency is increased by the fact that many acid survivors are not able to find work, due to impaired vision and range of motion. This negatively impacts their economic viability, causing hardships on the families/spouses that care for them. As a result, divorce rates are high, with abandonment by husbands.

CASE STUDIES OF ACID ATTACK VICTIMS

The researcher has highlighted some well known cases where girls and women have become victims of acid attack and how their life had been changed where they feel themselves as worst than handicapped and being dependent upon others. The pathetic condition of few acid attack victims are narrated below —

Case of Tapasi

A woman named Tapasi in her mid-30s was attacked with acid by a youth in Baduria, North 24-Pargana, on January 12, 2014 night. She has been admitted to a hospital with acid burn injuries. Atul Mondal, who lives in the same locality in Baduria's Kashpur, has allegedly been trying to woo the woman, who is a mother of two. According to police, the two knew each other. However, the woman has been trying to ignore Atul, since, the past few days as he was allegedly pressuring the woman to elope with him. Atul allegedly called the woman out of home at 8.30 p.m. on Sunday pleading that he wanted to iron out differences. Once the duo reached Kaharpara, about a kilometre away from the woman's house, he reportedly started forcing the woman to elope with him right away. On being refused, he allegedly poured acid on the woman. Local rushed to the spot on hearing the cries of the woman. Atul managed to flee. She was first rushed to Baduria State General Hospital from where she was shifted to a nursing home in Barasat (*The Times of India*, 2014:3).

Case of Meena Soni

Meena survived 75 per cent burns on her face and upper body. Her culprit was her husband. He had done it to her after about fifteen years of togetherness. Things were never normal between them. She belonged to a family from Lucknow and her husband lived in a town in Banda. She was the youngest among seven sibling and her parents married her off when she was just 16. She had just done her class 10. Her husband was a jewellery artist. The entire family was engaged in gold and silver jewellery making. But soon after marriage, he quit work. She had two daughters by then and no income to feed. Things became difficult to manage and she had to move out to earn the living. He was very unwilling, but she had no other option. He was suffering from tuberculosis and could not go out to work.

Meena Soni joined *Mahila Samakhya* and gradually became a reporter at *Khabar Lehariya*, the all-women newspaper of Banda and Chitrakoot. Her husband health improved, but he had lost all interest in work. Living on her earning had become his habit. He did not want to work and stopped her from going out of the house. She was working entire day, look after the family and every day they had arguments in the house. He put allegations on her and said that she should not go out to work. But that was not possible for her. Had she not worked, her children would have died of hunger. She was a reporter and people of the area recognised her for her work.

It was a summer morning of 2004 and she was fast asleep. Her children were playing outside the house. Her husband came with a bottle of acid and threw it on her face. She woke-up instantly. The burning sensation was strong enough to make her realise that she had faced an acid attack. She asked her daughter to call the rickshaw and ask him to take her to the doctor. God gave her extraordinary strength that day and she went to the hospital all alone. Thankfully, the doctor she went to was the same whom she had interviewed the previous day. He recognised her and gave her the treatment right way. She was in hospital when she came to know that her husband had attempted suicide. May be he was scared of the consequences that would have followed. Both of them were critical state and were shifted to the Allahabad medical college. He died on the fifth day and she stayed at the hospital for about three months, getting treated for the 75 per cent burns on her face, chest and hands. Her children were sent to her in-law house. The NGOs that she worked with supported her in all possible ways. They got her the entire medical assistant that she needed. Finally, she was back, but in a different shape. She stayed away from her children for two years as she worried that if they looked at her; they would get scared and might not come near her. Then she underwent another surgery at Lucknow and got her children back after two years (*The Hindustan Times*, 2013:9).

Case of Chanchal Kumari

Chanchal Kumari has dream of becoming computer engineer at the age of 18 years. She was encouraged by to pursue her dream by her father, Sailesh Paswan. A daily wage construction worker, who barely earns enough to make the two ends meet for his family of four, so unmindful of his meagre earning, he enrolled Chanchal in an Intermediate College and encouraged to do coaching for clearing engineering entrance examination.

Life was never easy, but the hope of a rewarding future kept her going. Trips from her native Chitnawan village, under Maner police station of Patna district (Bihar), to her college and coaching institute in Danapur were endless. Then, late in the night of October 21, 2012, her whole world came crashing around her. A few minutes short of midnight, four youth from her village climbed onto the roof of her single-storey *Indira Awas Yojana* house at Chitnawan, as she was sleeping there with her younger sister, Sonam. Two of them held her hands and the other two intruders poured almost a litre of acid on her face. As she writhed in agony, they laughed at her. One of them said: "Now you see we do whatever we say". These boys had been harassing her for months. They used to pass vulgar remarks, pull her *chunni* and follow her on their bike when she went to Danapur for her classes.

For months after the incident, nobody came to help victim family. Even the local *mukhia* (village headman) and the area MLA avoided visiting the families as the culprit are from a dominant community. Since then, internet campaigns by several NGOs and Maner based social activists have had many people pledging their support for my treatment and rehabilitation. Scheduled Caste Commission had given two sisters ₹ 2.42 lakh which was not enough to begin with, is long gone.

Chanchal want exemplary punishment to be handed out to the culprits, so that, it dissuades others like them from ruining the lives of innocent girls, who are pursuing their dream under trying circumstances (*The Hindustan Times*, 2013:10).

Case of Laxmi

Laxmi was from a poor family. Her father worked as a chef in a South Delhi home. She became friends with another girl in the neighbourhood and her brother soon started proposing her, she politely turned down his offer of marriage. She was only 15 and he, 32 years old. On April 22, 2005, she was waiting for a bus in a crowded Central Delhi area in daylight. He approached her with his brother's girl friend. Before she knew it, they had flung her onto road, pinned her down and threw acid on her face. In thirty seconds, the acid had leached through to her bones, melted her ear and reduced her face to a mass of third degree burn. The pain was unbearable. It happened in broad daylight at a busy bus stop, but no one answer her screams for help. A politician's driver took her to a hospital, where she was to stay for ten weeks. She learnt to live with the physical pain but what hurt more was the way society reacted. Her own relatives stopped seeing her, as did her friends. She stayed indoors for eight years and ventured out only in a *ghungat*. Since then, she has mostly lived indoors. She has had seven surgeries and needs four more. Life has been all about pain and rejection (*The Hindustan Times*, 2013:7).

Case of Preeti Rathi

Preeti passed her class 10 examination from National Public School in Narela (Delhi) and class 12 from the Narela Government School. Then she joined a four years nursing course at Laxmi Bai Batra College in Delhi and parents spent ₹ 5 lakh on her course. She graduated in 2011 with a first division. When her siblings were in school, Preeti helped them with their studies to save on tuition fee. After she cleared the course, Preeti did a year's internship at the Batra Hospital in Delhi and then joined the Susheela Hospital in Narela at a salary of ₹ 15,000. With her first salary, she brought new clothes for family members. Her starting salary at Naval Hospital would have been ₹ 40,000 plus allowances. The day before she left for Mumbai, she said she would take family members there once she got an official accommodation.

On May 1, 2013 Preeti along with her father, uncle and aunt boarded the Garib Rath Express from New Delhi for Mumbai to report at INHS Asvini. The train reached the Bandra station on time. They were looking for the nearest exit when someone tapped Preeti's shoulder from behind. She turned around. A man, his face half covered with a handkerchief, then threw acid on her face. Her father heard Preeti's scream, but before he could react, the culprit fled. A few drops of acid fell on her father's hand also. For a few minutes the three stood there paralysed, shocked by the sudden turn of events. Then they started shouting for help and asked around for the first-aid counter. There was none. She was shifted to the Masina Hospital in Byculla (East), which has a state-of-the-art burns centre. The hospital set-up 12 member's panel to plan her treatment, but her health had deteriorated by then. Her eyes were damaged, her kidneys were infected and acid had entered her oesophagus, windpipe and trachea.

She could not succumb to acid injury and died. After Preetis death, family members met Maharashtra Home Minister R.R. Patil and pressed for an investigation by Central Bureau of Investigation (CBI). The State Government agreed, but Union Government is still pending the file. For the family members, life has changed completely after Preeti's death (*The Hindustan Times*, 2013:10).

Case of Sabina Khatun

Like any other 18 years old, she was bubbly and full of zest for life. Every morning, she used to look forward to see her friends at school and her boy friend after the classes got over. Love is a beautiful feeling and it nourished her life. Isha Mondal and Sabina Khatun had been in a relationship for the past three years. Isha is a second year student at Fakir Chand College in Diamond Harbour (WB) and belong to her neighbouring village Kamarpole Dighipara. On the ill fated day, like any other day, she met him after school. Suddenly, he was struck by this whimsicality to marry her right away. Initially, she was taken aback by his insistence, but ultimately relented. Truth be told, she wanted to spend the rest of her life with him anyway. Isha took me home around 9.30 p.m. to meet his parents. Right from the beginning she could sense that his parents did not like her. They curtly asked her why she was visiting them so late at night. She plainly told them that their son had brought her to meet them to discuss our marriage. At this, Isha's parents told her to get out of his life but she tried to reason with them that they loved each other and wanted to get married. Isha's infuriated parents and brother, Insan and Iqbal, then started beating her up. She tried to fight back and save herself. Hearing the commotion, some neighbours rushed to their house. They enquired from Isha's family who she was and what an unknown girl like her was doing at their house so late at night.

It was almost 10 p.m. by then. Isha's father Iliyas told the neighbours that it was a family matter and they would settle it themselves. The neighbours then left, telling Iliyas not to hit Sabina and advice him to send her back to her parent home. But Iliyas convinced them that there was no problem and that Sabina would spend the night with Isha's mother. But the torture manifold after the neighbours went away. Isha's mother was now openly exhorting her husband and son to kill Sabina. She was already bleeding at the mouth from the beating received at their hands. Suddenly, Insan and Iqbal pinned her down to a chair and Iliyas fetched a bottle of acid. Insan was keeping her hand down and Iqbal held her cheeks, forcing her to open her mouth. Iliyas then emptied the acid bottle in her throat and forced his hand inside Sabina mouth, compelling her to swallow the burning liquid. All this while, Isha just watching and did not utter a single word in her defence. Sabina was left to fend for herself in the face of assault by the three men. She starting vomiting and soon fell unconscious. Fearing that Sabina might die, Isha's family dumped her at the Diamond Harbour Sub-divisional Hospital. The following morning, she was referred to the Chittaranjan Cancer Hospital at Hazra in Kolkata. She had suffered 20 per cent burns on her face, arms, chest and other parts of the body.

Sabina's father registered an FIR against Iliyas, Insan and Iqbal. But police picked up only Insan and kept him in the lock-up for a couple of days, after which he was bailed out. Her father requested a speedy trial and punishment for the guilty. The case is still pending in court. Throughout this trauma, the Association for Protection of Democratic Rights helped Sabina's family members with legal counselling and also took up the matter with the West Bengal Women's Commission and police. But Sabina's family members' grievances have not been redressed till date (*The Hindustan Times*, 2013:2).

Case of Annu Mukherjee

She came to Delhi when she was three. Her father was a lawyer and mother, a home-maker. Her parents had decided that Annu should live with her childless aunt. Annu stayed with aunt in Mehrauli, where she studied in a Bengali school. She loved dancing and studying. Her parents died when she was 11 years and her brother, Kaushal, was barely two months old at that time. Her uncle never let her meet or see them. The aunt had proved to be cruel women and she found solace in two neighbourhood friends — Seema and Sapna. When it becomes impossible to live with her aunt, she moved in with them. She had to stop studying and start working to sustain her brother and her.

One day, they come across an advertisement in the *Punjab Kesari*. Rajdoot, a South Delhi hotel, was looking for girls to dance in their variety show. Annu applied and got selected. A woman named Meena Khan, a mother of two who did not earn much, was among her co-workers. One day she asked Annu to leave the job. Annu told her, "This is all she can do to earn a living, she cannot leave". She went to police to file a complaint but the hotel owner threatened her that she would lose her job if she pressed charges against her. Meena apologised and she let the matter go.

Around 6.30 p.m. on December 19, 2004, she was heading for her duty and her brother was at the tuition. The hotel used to send a vehicle to pick her up and it was waiting. As she walked out, she saw Meena, her brother Qayoom Khan and some of their friends. The winter chill had just set in and they were covered in shawls. She asked Meena what they were doing there and she said in a strange tone: "*Bas tujhse milne aayi hu*". In a flash, her brother drew out an arm and threw acid on her. She screamed in shock and pain, and the passersby started pouring water and milk on me. Her cloths got burnt and her chest was exposed. An auto driver immediately covered her with his shirt and took her to Appollo Hospital. Later she was shifted to AIIMS where the word "treatment" took an altogether different meaning. She came home after spending three months in the hospital. Her brother was 13 years old and everything was over for them. She went through seven surgeries that cost her ₹ 2-3 lakh. She still needs another ₹ 20 lakh to get better. Eventually, the money ran out and so did her treatment.

She pursued the case in court. That was a new battle. Our justice system is slow, but she finally won the case. Meena and her brother were penalised by Court. But today, they are out of jail and roaming freely. Annu's life stands ruined. Her brother had to stop studying so that he could support her (*The Hindustan Times*, 2013:1).

Case of Haseena Hussain

Haseena Hussain is officially the first acid attack victim in Karnataka. April 20, 1999, was the day she was disfigured by a plastic jug full of sulphuric acid when a satanic man prevailed over God reworked her face and fate. It was also the day her soul died to live in hell. She lost everything that day, including her eyes.

Before her world turned dark, she had completed a computer course while studying for the first year B.Com. She got a job at a software centre run by a former Indian Air Force employee, Joseph Rodriguez. After the centre incurred heavy losses, she left it and joined another office. Joseph wanted her to return and work at a computer set-up in his house, but she rejected his offer. Joseph was obstinate. He kept pestering her with his offer. He simply refused to believe that she could not really want to return to his employment. Joseph was furious to his or her employment; he threatened her with dire consequences for not accepting his offer.

That fateful day, she left her house at Jalahalli (Bengaluru North-East) for office; suddenly a motorcycle-born man splashed the liquid content of a plastic jug on her and sped away. The liquid which was later confirmed as sulphuric acid made her face, eyes, neck, chest, hands, legs and clothes burnt. It was as if someone had set her on fire. She cried out in excruciating pain. Some people standing nearby immediately moved her to HMT Hospital and from there to Ramaiah and finally to Victoria Hospital.

She underwent a series of painful surgeries, each one lasting five to seven hours. The nose surgery was particularly agonising and it took at least 10 hours. But nothing could make her see again, inspite bearing each of the psychological pain. She was on bed rest virtually for 10 years. During this period, her parents suffered a lot and had to even sell their house for her treatment. Her father a retired Government employee and her homemaker mother were initially not in a position to bear the expensive treatment and she was, therefore, treated in Government hospital for eight months. Even today, she cannot sit straight, walk without support. She hides her eyes behind black goggles that had dreamt of a bright life. A five-year criminal trial in a lower court gave her attacker five years three months jail, beside a fine of ₹ 3 lakh. He was convicted only for causing grievous hurt and not attempt to murder, the Bangalore High Court later sentenced him to life imprisonment for attempt to murder and awarded her ₹ 2 lakh. The Supreme Court later upheld the High Court order (*The Hindustan Times*, 2013:10).

LEGAL REMEDIES

The Indian Parliament has passed the Criminal Law (Amendment) Act 2013, with special provisions for acid victim. For the first time, acid attacks have been included under a standalone provision in the Indian Penal Code (IPC). It lays down two Sections, namely 326A (Voluntarily causing grievous hurt by use of acid, etc.) and 326B (Voluntarily throwing or attempting to throw acid) be added to the IPC (GoI, 2013).

> **Section 326A** of the Indian Penal Code stated that whoever causes permanent or partial damage or deformity to, or burn or maims or disfigures or disables, any part of the body of a person or causes grievous hurt by throwing acid on or by administering acid to that person, or by using any other means with the intention of causing or with the knowledge that he is likely to cause such injury or hurt, shall be punished with imprisonment of either description for a term which shall not be less than ten years but which may extend to imprisonment for life, and with fine:

Provided that such fine shall be just and reasonable to meet the medical expenses of the treatment of the victim:

Provided further that any fine imposed under this section shall be paid to the victim.

Section 326B of the Indian Penal Code stated that whoever throws or attempts to throw acid on any person or attempts to administer acid to any person, or attempts to use any other means, with the intention of causing permanent or partial damage or deformity or burns or maiming or disfigurement or disability or grievous hurt to that person, shall be punished with imprisonment of either description for a term which shall not be less than five years but which may extend to seven years, and shall also be liable to fine.

Supreme Court Verdict

In the wake of increasing acid attacks on girls and women, the Supreme Court on 18th July, 2013 directed that the crime be made a non-bailable offence and enhanced to ₹ 3 lakh the compensation amount for victims, even as it banned over the counter sale of the corrosive at retail outlets without maintenance of record of stock and buyers' identity.

The direction came from a Bench headed by Justice R.M. Lodha while asking States and Union Territories to frame rules to regulate sale of acids and other corrosive substance within three months. On rehabilitation, the Bench observed that the amount which is being paid is "grossly inadequate". The compensation amount for after-care and rehabilitation cost at present ranges between ₹ 5000 and ₹ 1,50,000. "It cannot be overlooked that acid attack victims need to undergo a series of plastic surgeries and other corrective treatment. We accordingly direct that the acid attack victims shall be paid a compensation of at least of ₹ 3 lakh by the State Government concerned as an after-care and rehabilitation cost for such victims", the Court said. The Bench said an acid attack victim would be paid ₹ 1 lakh within 15 days of the incident and "the balance of ₹ 2 lakh shall be paid by the State or Union Territory concerned as expeditiously as possible and positively within two months of the incident." The compliance of the order has to be ensured by the Chief Secretaries of the State and administrators of the UTs, respectively (*The Times of India*, 2013:1).

"Over the counter sale of acid is completely prohibited unless the seller maintains a log/register recording the details of the persons to whom acid is sold, the quantity sold and shall contain the address of the person to whom it is sold", the Court said in an interim order. The Apex

Court said violation of its directions "shall attract prosecution under the Poisons Act, 1919" and "the Sub Divisional Magistrate (SDM) shall be vested with the responsibility of fining the violators and initiating prosecution".

The Bench was hearing a Public Interest Litigation (PIL) filed in 2006 by a Delhi-based acid attack victim Laxmi who was then a minor. It also passed a slew of interim direction on various issues, including sale of acids. The Court said States would frame the rules regulating the sale of acid within three months after the receipt of model rules from the Central Government. Educational institutions, research laboratories and hospitals "shall maintain a register of usage of acid and file the same with local police and the Sub Divisional Magistrate (SDM)", the Judges said (*The Statesman*, 2013:4).

The Apex Court had on July 16, 2013 issued detailed directions to all State Governments and Union Territories to frame rules within three months for regulating the sale of acid. However, after repeated lapses of the deadline and only Bihar, Jammu & Kashmir and Pondicherry making some headway, the Supreme Court issued fresh directives on December 3, 2013 to all States and Union Territories to frame rules on acid sale by March of 2014 (*Sunday Times of India*, 2014:7).

The Supreme Court on 10 April, 2015 directed private hospitals to provide free treatment, including specialised surgeries, to acid attack victims and asked Government authorities to take action against them if fail to comply with its order.

It had directed States to implement norms for retail sale of acid, treating it as poison under the Poisons Act, 1919, within three months. The Court had banned sale of acid to minors and said the corrosive substance could be sold only to those with identity cards issued by the Government and who could specify the purpose for the purchase in writing. It had also asked the Centre and States to make acid attack offences non-bailable (*The Times of India*, 2014:13).

The Supreme Court on December 7, 2015 asked State Government to treat acid attack survivors as disabled persons to enable them to get benefits of reservation in government jobs and other social welfare schemes (*The Times of India*, 2015:8).

High Court Decision

Expressing concern over increasing number of acid attacks, Punjab and Haryana High Court on July 27, 2013 stated that the Court intends to fast-track all such cases pending before subordinate courts. "We have called for informations from the districts concerned regarding pending cases involving acid attacks," observed Chief Justice Sanjay Kishan Kaul while hearing an acid attack case. The High Court had taken *suo motu* cognizance of acid attack on Mandeep Kaur and her father Shamsher Singh on July 11, 2013 while they were on way to Moga District Court to attend hearing of a case.

The Delhi Government has directed all the Government and private hospitals in the National Capital Territory to provide "immediate and free" medical treatment to the victims of acid attack. The hospitals are also directed to ensure no patient returns without first aid and if the concerned hospital does not have the advanced medical facilities for treatment in such cases, they should refer it to other hospitals after giving the primary aid. "Duty is cast on every hospital management that no victims of acid attack will be returned without providing the victim first aid or immediate medical treatment" (*The Pioneer*, 2014).

Role of NGOs

Many NGOs have risen in the areas with the highest occurrence of acid attacks. In India there are so many non-profit organisations, which offer acid victims legal, medical, counselling, and monetary assistance in rebuilding their lives.

Acid Survivors Foundation India (ASFI) purports to be the leading NGO in India for prevention of acid burn violence as well as for providing support services to survivors through a network of chapters and partners by sharing knowledge, expertise and best practices. ASFI acts as a forum for advocacy of acid related causes, endeavours to promote a social environment conducive to elimination of all forms of gender violence and espouses a firm legal basis for prosecution of offenders and prescription of national guidelines for treatment, aftercare and rehabilitation of acid survivors. Acid Survivors Trust India (AST-IND) was established in perpetuity at Kolkata as a registered non-profit organisation.

Acid Survivors Foundation (ASF) was formed in 1999 with the growing concern of the rising trend of acid violence in Bangladesh. Acid violence is a form of gender based violence that reflects and perpetuates the inequality of women in society. This form of violence cuts across cultural and religious barriers and impede on women's right to fully participate in society. It has the effect of denying women's important rights such as economic well-being, social well-being, political participation, personal fulfilment and self-worth.

The Campaign and Struggle Against Acid Attacks on Women (CSAAAW), a registered non-profit trust, has been operating as a coalition of women's rights organisations and media activist groups that are based largely out of Bangalore, since 2003. In January 2004, the CSAAAW had organised a public hearing where women acid attack survivors and their families had shared testimonies of the inhuman actions that they had endured. The campaign also brought out a comprehensive report, titled 'Burnt but not defeated', which has captured in detail the date, time and place of various incidents, the personal details such as name, age, occupation, information regarding the family, the aftermath of the episode in terms of the duration and type of medical treatment and the expenditure.

Acid Survivors Trust International (ASTI) is the only organisation whose sole purpose is to work towards the end of acid violence across the world. Recognising the need for local knowledge and expertise in order to combat acid violence effectively.

To tackle this problem, acid attack survivor Shirin Juwaley set-up an NGO in Mumbai called Palash Foundation. The Palash Foundation was formed in an effort to socially and economically re-integrate people with disfigurement. *Disfigurement* is defined by Palash Foundation as an altered physical appearance which can be congenital, due to accidents, burn injuries, surgical intervention, skin deformities, illnesses or any other reason.

Suggestions

- In most acid attack cases, the victim does not die, but her face and life is ruined. Hence, acid attacks must be dealt separately and specifically and must be categorised under heinous crime. There should be minimum sentence to be life imprisonment.
- Acid attack is a cruel and inhumane crime, which calls for immediate medical treatment to the victim, irrespective of court's decisions. But, the present laws do not stand sufficient, as many victims are exhausted with running around courts for years together after having to brave a life-long health complication because of the chemical injuries they sustain. Along with specific laws to deal with acid attack cases, there must be a provision for fast track courts too, where cases are solved within three months.
- Protection officers to deal with threats and potential risks to women's safety must be appointed to stop acid attacks.

- Acid attack victims must be given complete legal support to ensure they do not have to struggle a lot to get justice.
- The women victims of acid attacks mainly face the struggle of expensive surgeries, which hinders their appropriate and speedy treatment. Hence, government must take the responsibility of their treatment.
- The physical and psychological trauma following an acid attack makes life very difficult for the victims. The government must take steps to rehabilitate acid attack survivors with counselling and other provisions.

Conclusion

Thus, the process of justice to acid attack victims remains incomplete until acid attack survivors get immediate medical, legal and economic help along with the social acceptance. It is not possible to ban the sale of acid in country. Acid is needed for construction work, painting and other commercial activities. What needs to be changed is the mindset and attitude of the society as acid attacks are a manifestation of gender discrimination. Government officials and police should be sensitive in dealing with acid attack survivors. People should be sensitive enough to give company to or be seen with a burn of acid attack victims. The perpetrators must be tried quickly and punished severely. And the survivors must automatically qualify for a monthly pension, concessions in using public transports, reservations in higher education and employment and other benefits similar to those given to people with disabilities so that the survivors can try to lead a normal life.

REFERENCES

Anway, Afroza, 2003. "Acid Violence and Medical Care in Bangladesh: Women's Activism as Care Work", *Gender & Society*, April, Vol. 17, No. 2, pp. 305-13.

GoI, 2013. "The Criminal Law (Amendment) Act".

Radhika, Coomaraswamy, 2005. "Human Security and Gender Violence", *Economic and Political Weekly*, October 29, Vol. X, pp. 33-47.

Sunday Times of India, 2014. "Worst Sex Ratio States Lead in Acid Attacks", January 12, Kolkata, p. 7.

The Hindu, 2013. "Stop Acid Violence", March 15, New Delhi.

The Hindustan Times, 2013. "Acid Attack Kills 28 Years Old in MP", July 23, Kolkata, p. 9.

The Hindustan Times, 2013. "Acid Survivors Wants Us to Fight for Them", July 22, Kolkata, p. 1.

The Hindustan Times, 2013. "Don't Stare at Me: I am Human Too", July 22, Kolkata, p. 7.

The Hindustan Times, 2013. "I Was Seen Only as a Commodity", July 24, Kolkata, p. 10.

The Hindustan Times, 2013. "I can't Even Cry Anymore", July 25, Kolkata, p. 10.

The Hindustan Times, 2013. "My Face was Used to Settle Scores", July 26, Kolkata, p. 10.

The Hindustan Times, 2013. "Till Death, She Just Kept Asking Why?", July 27, Kolkata, p. 10.

The Hindustan Times, 2013. "They Emptied an Acid Bottle in my Throat", July 28, Kolkata, p. 2.

The Hindustan Times, 2013. "SC Curbs Acid Sale, Order More Money for Victims", July 20, Kolkata, p. 1.

The Hindustan Times, 2013. "Stop Acid Attack", July 23, Kolkata, p. 9.

The Hindustan Times, 2013. "Stop Acid Attacks", July 31, Kolkata, p. 10.

The Pioneer, 2014. "Treat Acid Attack, Rape Victims For Free: Government", January 24, New Delhi.

The Statesman, 2013. "SC Bans Over the Counter Acid Sale", July 19, Kolkata, p. 4.

The Statesman, 2013. "Woman Dies After Acid Attack", July 22, Kolkata, p. 3.

The Times of India, 2013. "SC Increases Acid Attacks Payout to ₹ 3 Lakh", July 19, Kolkata, p. 1.

The Times of India, 2014. "Woman Burnt with Acid", January 14, Kolkata, p. 3.

The Times of India, 2015. "SC: Treat Acid Attack Victims as Disabled," December 7, Kolkata, p. 8.

The Times of India, 2015. "Treat Acid Attack Victims for Free: SC to Private Hospital", April 11, Kolkata, pp. 1 & 13.

Verma, Harish, 2013. "Acid Attacks Against Women in India: The Human Rights Perspective", *Indian Bar Review*, Vol. XL(2), pp. 81-95.

Websites

https://en.wikipedia.org/wiki/Acid_throwing
www.acidsurvivors.org
www.asfi.in
www.dnaindia.com
www.justiceforwomeninindia.com
www.legalindia.in
www.palashfoundation.org
www.stopacidattack.org
www.who.int

12

CHILD EDUCATION

"No subject is of greater importance than that of education. It is the men and women in a country that make and build a nation and it is education that is supposed to build those men and women."

Jawaharlal Nehru

Introduction

The education is generally perceived as a major input in the process of character building of students as well as a means for the inculcation of healthy social attitude. It is one of the channels to transform society. It is always said that education is the best virtue a man possesses. Education completes a human being giving a person temperance, tolerance and ability to realise his other rights. Education, according to UNICEF, is an inalienable, non-derogable right that is inextricably linked to other fundamental human rights and must be guaranteed to all children both in and outside of emergency situation. It is a powerful and empowering tool for the development of children to their full potential as well as to improve the lives of vulnerable and marginalised children, and is essential to promote the empowerment of the girl-child. Children are the nation's assets and future resources of manpower for the country. They constitute the core of human society. It is their development, which sustain the society. Their development with dignity is a matter of great concern. It has been recognised that elementary education is a fundamental component of education and the most significant part of the development process (Singh, 2010:102).Children's right to education has close link to their right to development. India being a party to the Convention on the Right of the Child, 1989, is committed to support development of children so as to promote their right to life under Article 21 of the Constitution of India. Education is a medium of exposure for a child to different points of view based on depiction of established facts (Tiwari, 2013:147).

FUNCTIONS OF EDUCATION FOR SOCIETY

According to Emile Durkheim, the major function of education is the transmission of society's norms and values. "Society can survive" he says, "only if there exists among its members a sufficient degree of homogeneity; education perpetuates and reinforces this homogeneity by fixing in the child from the beginning the essential similarities which collective life demands." A vitally important task for all society is to bring close together a mass of individuals into a united whole. The individuals must have a sense of belonging to society. Durkheim holds that education provides the necessary link between individuals and society by indoctrinating them with the values and ideals, traditions and thoughts of the community.

Secondly, Durkheim argues that the formal education imparted by schools cannot be provided either by the family or the peer groups. The family is a group of kins knit together by ties of blood. Family relationships are, therefore, coloured by love and affection, emotions and sentiments. One cannot, in the nature of things, look beyond one's family and get acquainted with the promise and problems of living in the large society. Peers are one's personal choice. Naturally, membership of peer group cannot prepare one for the large society. The school system, on the other hand, is a miniature society in which a pupil interacts with other members of the school community in terms of a fixed set of rules. In the words of Durkheim: "It is by respecting the school rules that child learns to respect rules in general, that he develops the habit of self-control can restrain himself. It is a first initiation into the austerity of duty. Serious life has now begun." In the words of Talcott Parsons, a family or a peer group upholds 'particularistic' standers whereas a school upholds 'universalistic' standers. Thus, the school prepares young people for their adult roles. Thirdly, Durkhiem argues that formal educational institutions, apart from transmitting general values which provide the 'necessary homogeneity for social survival', also transmit specific skills which provide the 'necessary diversity for social cooperation'. In pre-industrial societies, technical skills were imparted chiefly through the family and the occupational group in informal and practical ways. Thus, a child born in the family of a carpenter used to learn the skills of the trade informally from the members of his family. Industrial societies have become highly specialised and complex, calling for skill of a very high order. Complex division of labour, which is the defining feature of an industrial society, tends to strengthen social cohesion. This he calls organic solidarity. Industrial society is thus knit together by value consensus and a specialised division of labour which makes inter-dependence a condition for survival. Fourthly, the objective of education, as defined by Durkhiem, is "to awaken and develop in the child those physical, intellectual and moral states which are required of him by the milieu for which he is specially destined." By way of elaborating this statement of Durkhiem, Bottomore observes that "the function of education in preparing the child for a particular milieu in society . . . has traditionally meant preparing him for membership of a particular group in the social hierarchy. Social divisions exist in almost all societies. Wherever there is a system of social stratification, there is corresponding differentiation within the educational system. Class divisions are reflected in the educational system. In fact, education is used as an agency for preserving class privileges and interest and thereby maintaining class distinctions. Thus, in ancient India, the education of children belonging to higher castes was quite distinct from the education that was available for the great majority of the population. The education of the former was conducted by a hereditary priesthood, and it largely excluded secular instruction and was chiefly concerned with the transmission of religious doctrines and knowledge of the scriptures. With the establishment of British rule in India, the ancient educational system declined. But the introduction of English education tended to reinforce the separation of those who received English education from the society. Even after five decades of India's Independence, class distinctions are maintained by the existence of different types of schools for the various social groups. This kind of educational differentiation exists in all modern societies, however, much they may be committed to egalitarian policies. Fifthly, the importance of education as an agency of social control cannot be ignored. The major function of education, according to Durkhiem, is the transmissions of society norms and values by the older generations among those who are not yet ready for social life. Once a child internalises through intellectual exposure, the distinctive traits of this culture, his actions and behaviour patterns are moulded by his intellectual orientation. Conformity to social norms and values becomes easy and spontaneous. Links are firmly established between the society on the one hand and individuals on the other. Seen in this perspective, education appears to be a powerful and very effective agency of social control. The questions of applying social sanctions arises only when there are deviations or tendencies towards deviations from socially prescribed norms of behaviour. The application of social becomes unnecessary if educational agencies can transmit effectively society norms and values to individuals during impressionable periods of their lives.

We should note, however, that the effectiveness of normal education as a means of social control is diminished by certain factors in modern times. In earlier societies for example, literacy was valued so much so that it was the basis of prestige and power. The teachers also naturally enjoyed great respect and honour. Hence, it was not difficult for teachers to communicate to their pupils social traditions and values and to regulate their conduct in a manner consistent with the recognised code of the community. With the establishment of industrialised order, the scale of values has changed. Wealth and not education is the main determinant of one's status in modern industrialist societies. This has undermined the prestige of teachers to some extent. Moreover, the expansion of mass literacy in the modern world has also contributed to the decline of the prestige of teachers, for he is "no longer set part as the literate man". There is yet another fact contributing towards the same end. Now-a-days, the values professed by a teacher are no longer authoritative. They have "to compete with the values presented to the child by his family, peer group, and the media of mass communication." There is, therefore, the possibility of conflict between "different codes of behaviour and different agencies of social control in contemporary societies". For instance, India being wedded to the ideal of secularism, Indian schools do not provide for any religious instruction. In these circumstances, a boy or a girl who comes from a very conservative family with religious tradition, is likely to face conflicts between "secular character of state education as contrasted with the religious values of the family". We may conceive of innumerable cases of such conflicts among different agencies of social control.

UNICEF (India)

Despite a major improvement in literacy rates during the 1990s, the number of children who are not in school remains high. Gender disparities in education persist: far more girls than boys fail to complete primary school. The literacy rate jumped from 52 per cent in 1991 to 65 per cent in 2001. The absolute number of non-literates dropped for the first time and gross enrollment in Government-run primary schools increased from over 19 million in the 1950s to 114 million by 2001. 90 million females in India are non-literate but 20 per cent of children aged 6 to14 are still not in school and millions of women remain non-literate despite the spurt in female literacy in the 1990s. Several problems persist: issues of 'social' distance — arising out of caste, class and gender differences —

deny children equal opportunities. Child labour in some parts of the country and resistance to sending girls to school remain real concern. School attendance is improving: more children than ever between the ages of 6 and 14 are attending school across the country. The education system faces a shortage of resources, schools, classrooms and teachers. There are also concerns relating to teacher training, the quality of the curriculum, assessment of learning achievements and the efficacy of school management. Given the scarcity of quality schools, many children drop-out before completing five years of primary education; many of those who stay on learn little. Girls belonging to marginalised social and economic groups are more likely to drop-out of school at an early age. With one upper primary school for every three primary schools, there are simply not enough upper primary centres even for those children who complete primary school. For girls, especially, access to upper primary centres becomes doubly hard.

Education as means of empowerment of women can bring about a positive attitudinal change. It is, therefore, crucial for the socio-economic and political progress of India. Table 12.1 shows that female literacy rate is showing an increasing trend and both rural and urban female literacy rates are showing rising trend since1961.

Table 12.1: Literacy Rate in India

Year	*Literacy Rate*			*Female Literacy*	
	Total	*Male*	*Female*	*Rural*	*Urban*
1961	28.3	40.4	15.4	10.1	40.5
1971	34.5	46.0	22.0	15.5	48.8
1981	43.6	56.4	29.8	21.7	56.3
1991	52.2	64.1	39.3	30.6	64.1
2001	64.8	75.3	53.7	46.6	73.0
2011	72.9	80.9	64.6	58.8	80.0

Source: Census, RGI, GoI.

Government Scheme for Empowering Girls Through Education

Department of Education has initiated scheme to reduce the gender gap in the education of children through following programmes —

1. ***Early Child Care Education Centres (ECCE):*** These centres are set-up to ensure better enrollment and retention of girls in the primary schools. Since, the girl child has the responsibility to look after the young siblings and is, therefore, deprived of school education, an ECCE centre attached to the school would ensure

that girls would come to school. It is intended that if school going girls have access to such centres, they would get enrolled in school, and would be retained in schools. The scheme also envisages provision of good quality education to such girls. At the ECCE centres, the physical and psychological growth and development of all children in the 3-6 age group, is provided for. The education department at the district level has the responsibility for *Sarva Shiksha Abhiyan* and Department of Social Welfare (through the integrated child development services programme) has the responsibility for running the ECCE centres.

2. ***National Programme on Education for Girls at Elementary Level (NPEGEL):*** Since, education is a concurrent subject, this national programme is also being implemented at the State level in some selected districts and blocks since, 2003. It is intended to increase the enrollment rates of girls belonging to SC/ST communities at the elementary stage. The scheme intends to focus attention on the educationally deprived sections and to encourage the enrollment, retention and quality education of girls belonging to the SC/ST communities. It offers materials incentives such as stationary and introduces additional incentives like awards, remedial teaching and bridge courses as well as development of a model upper primary school in each cluster.
3. ***Kasturba Gandhi Balika Vidyalaya (KGBV):*** The scheme draws its legitimacy from the thrust in national policy documents as well as international discourse that refers to bridging the 'gender gap'. Following this thrust, the scheme is being implemented in educationally backward blocks with a wider gender gap. The scheme is intended for girls belonging to the Scheduled Castes (SCs), Scheduled Tribes (STs), Other Backward Classes (OBCs), religious minorities and Below Poverty Line (BPL) households. Funded by the Government of India, under the Sarva Shiksha Abhiyan, the basic idea behind the scheme is to give a second chance for mainstreaming rural girls belonging to deprived social backgrounds who could not study up to or beyond class V. The second opportunity consists of the facility to stay in a hostel while studying for the upper primary stage of elementary education, namely classes VI to VIII. They are set-up in areas where there are minimum of 50 school going girls who are school drop-outs. As all the girls are primary school drop-outs, they are above 10 years of age and are mostly in their teens.

4. ***Innovative Scheme for the Adolescent Girls:*** In order to create and sustain the interest of girls in education, they are trained to produce items that can be used in their daily lives. They are also offered components of empowerment strategies such as personal development, confidence building abilities, and life skills oriented education.
5. ***Mahila Samakhya (Education for Women's Equality)*** was the first major scheme launched by the Central Government that owned its genesis to the National Policy on Education (1986) recognising the empowering potential of education and education as an agent of basic change in the status of women. The basic objectives of Mahila Samakhya are:

   (a) As a gender-based programme, to create an ambience in the society for tolerance and mutual respect for women.

   (b) To ensure that education becomes accessible to the socially and economically marginalised women and girls.

   (c) To encourage and promote a gender-based discourse in society.

   (d) To enhance the self-image and self-confidence of women and enable them to critically analyse their role as individual women and as members of society so that they can begin to challenge that role collectively and initiate a process of social change.

   (e) To collectively participate in decision-making and seek equal rights and opportunities for a more egalitarian society.

   (f) To enhance participation of women and girls in formal education programmes. Education Department of the Ministry of Human Resource Development, Government of India launched Mahila Samakhya as a major programme for bringing about women's development as well as empowerment in 1989 on a pilot basis in 6 States of India, with funding from the Netherlands Government (Sharma, 2015:7).

CONSTITUTIONAL MANDATE

The amendment in the Constitution of India includes the Right to Education in the list of Fundamental Rights. The inclusion of this right within the scope of Article 21 (the right to life and personal liberty) only underscores its importance.

The Right of Children to Free and Compulsory Education Act 2009

The Right of Children to Free and Compulsory Education Act 2009 (popularly called The Right to Education Act or RTE Act) was approved by the Cabinet on 2nd July, 2009. The Rajya Sabha passed the Bill on 20th July, 2009, and the Lok Sabha on 4th August, 2009. It received Presidential Assent on the 26th August and was published for general information in the Gazette of India on the 27th August, 2009. The Act describes the modalities of the provision of the free and compulsory education for children between the age of 6 and 14 in India under Article 21A of the Constitution of India.

The main objects of the Right of Children to Free and Compulsory Education Act 2009 are —

1. To provide free and compulsory education to all children of India in the 6 to 14 age group.
2. To provide for pre-school education to prepare children above that age of three for elementary education and to provide early childhood care and education for all children until they complete the age of six years.
3. That no child admitted in a school shall be held back in any class or expelled from school till the completion of elementary education.
4. That a child who completes elementary education shall be awarded a certificate.
5. To provide of a fixed student-teacher ratio.
6. To provide for 25 per cent reservation for economically disadvantaged communities in admission to class one in all private schools.
7. To provide that no capitation fee and screening procedure for admission.
8. To ensure good quality elementary education conforming to the standards and norms specified in the Schedule.
9. To ensure adequate professional degree for school teachers within five years.
10. To provide that school infrastructure (where there is problem) to be improved in three years, else recognition cancelled.
11. To provide that financial burden will be shared by State and Central Governments.
12. To provide that no child shall be subject to physical punishment or mental harassment.

13. To provide for the duty of every parent or guardian to admit the child to a neighbourhood school for elementary education and that no child should be denied admission for lack of age proof.
14. To provide that the National Commission for Elementary Education shall be constituted to monitor all aspects for elementary education including quality.
15. To provide that no teacher shall engage himself or herself in private tuition or private teaching activity.
16. To ensure that availability of a neighbourhood school for providing free and compulsory education for every child within a period of three years from commencement of this Act.
17. To provide that the medium of instruction shall, as far as practicable, be in child's mother tongue.

Suggestion to Make RTE Act Effective

1. Government will prescribe minimum infrastructure requirements for schools to maintain quality of schools. The States will identify schools that do not conform to such requirements and will require them to maintain quality within three years or face derecognition.
2. Parents to constitute seventy five per cent of the members in school management committee of which 50 per cent to be woman members.
3. Schools whether private or Government will have common minimum standards have playgrounds, drinking water, library and toilets.
4. Schools will maintain 1:40 teacher student ratio.
5. Any school which fails to fulfil the prescribed norms, the recognition of it would be withdrawn and if any person still continue to run the school, he/she would be liable to pay the fine up to one lakh rupees (Gupta, 2013:37).
6. Enhance funding for school education. India's spending of 3.1 per cent of GDP on education is one of the lowest in the world and there is a huge shortfall in the funding required for achieving RTE norms.
7. The entire academic support structure for teachers needs to be revitalised and focused on the vision of classroom change.
8. Strengthen educational administration and school monitoring to make it more responsive to the demand of RTE.

9. Invest in continuous teacher professional development. The quality of pre-service and in-service teacher training is highly unsatisfactory. Teacher needs high quality professional learning opportunities relevant to classroom teaching. In addition, regular academic discussion support system is in disarray and burdened with administrative tasks.
10. Put in place policies and system that ensure that teachers are posted to school those need them (Jhingram, 2014:6).

UNIVERSAL DECLARATION OF HUMAN RIGHTS (UDHR)

Everyone has the right to education. This right is explicitly stated in the United Nations' Universal Declaration of Human Rights (UDHR), adopted in 1948. The UDHR provides —

1. Everyone has the right to education. Education shall be free, at least in the elementary and fundamental stages. Elementary education shall be compulsory. Technical and professional education shall be made generally available and higher education shall be equally accessible to all on the basis of merit.
2. Education shall be directed to the full development of the human personality and to the strengthening of respect for human rights and fundamental freedoms.
3. Parents have a prior right to choose the kind of education that shall be given to their children. (UDHR, Article 26).

CONVENTION ON THE RIGHTS OF THE CHILD (CRC)

CRC has some detailed provisions on the educational rights of the child. They are —

1. State Parties recognise the right of the child to education, and with a view to achieving this right progressively and on the basis of equal opportunity:

    - Make primary education compulsory and available free to all;
    - Encourage the development of different forms of secondary education, including general and vocational education, make them available and accessible to every child, and take appropriate measures such as the introduction of free

education and offering financial assistance in case of need;

- Make higher education accessible to all on the basis of capacity by every appropriate means;
- Make education and vocational information and guidance available and accessible to all children;
- Take measures to encourage regular attendance at school and the reduction of drop-out rates.

2. State Parties shall take all appropriate measures to ensure that school discipline is administered in a manner consist with the child's human dignity and in conformity with the present Convention.
3. State Parties shall promote and encourage international cooperation in matter relating to education, in particular with a view to contributing to the elimination of ignorance and illiteracy throughout the world and facilitating access to scientific and technical knowledge and modern teaching method. In this regard, particular account shall be taken of the needs of developing countries (CRC, Article 28).

Conclusion

The basic aim of child education is to equip child with basic minimum levels of knowledge, attitude, value, and skills so to start the journey of one's life. To make education more meaningful for the children of India, emphasis must shift for vocational as well as continuous provision of education, so that, they can also share the gain of our increasing GDP and not remain aloof from the fruit of development. The decision of the Supreme Court of India and the enactment of the Right of Children to Free and Compulsory Education Act 2009 are aids to fulfil the constitutional objectives of free and compulsory education to every child, but the task is enormous. Only policy-making is not sufficient for its success, unless it is implemented properly. The purpose of free and compulsory education is to provide a child enhanced awareness, greater openness, the courage to question, perseverance in searching for solutions and living in society with dignity. The right to education is a fundamental human right. Every individual, irrespective of race, gender, nationality is entitled to free elementary education. Education should be free at least in the elementary stage. Ensuring access to education is a precondition for full realisation of the right to education. In a country of desparate access to education, it is very critical that State takes all necessary measures to impart quality education to its future generation. As Mahatma Gandhi rightly observed: "*By education I mean an all-round drawing out of the best in child and man — body, mind and spirit. Literacy is not the end of education or even the beginning.*"

REFERENCES

Banerjee, Amit, 2013. "Educational Intervention for the Marginalised Children: A Critical Appraisal", *All India Reporter*, January.

Gupta, Suman and Shridul Gupta, 2013. "The Right of Children to Free and Compulsory Education Act 2009 — Fulfilment of a Dream for Millions of Children", *Nyaya Deep*, Vol. XIV, July-October, p. 37.

Jhingram, Dhir, 2014."There are no Quick-fixes", *The Hindustan Times*, June 23.

Mishra, D.N., 2013. "Need for Strong Legislation in India for Unborn Child and Child Education in Global Context", *Indian Bar Review*, Vol. XL(3).

Nayar, Usha, 1989. *Education of the Child in India with Focus on the Girl Child*, NCERT, New Delhi.

Rao, K. Surekha, 2007. "Education as a Strategy for Women's Empowerment", *Women's Link*, Vol. 13, No. 1, January-March.

Sharma, Arpita, 2015. "*Beti Bachao, Beti Padhao* Programme: An Eagle's View", *Kurukshetra*, March, Vol. 63, No. 5.

Singh, Banshi Dhar, 2010. "Right to Child Education", *Nyaya Deep*, Vol. XI, Issue 2, April, pp, 102-12.

The Right of Children to Free and Compulsory Education Act 2009.

Tiwari, Shraddha, 2013. "Right to Education as Human Rights", *Indian Bar Review*, Vol. XL(3).

UNICEF, 1990. *Children and Women in India: A Situational Analysis*, UNICEF, New Delhi.

UNICEF, 1985. *Data Sheet on Health: The Girl Child in India*, UNICEF, New Delhi.

website

www.unicef.org

13

TRAFFICKING IN CHILD FOR PROSTITUTION

Introduction

Trafficking in children is one of the worst and most brazen abuses violating the rights of women and child. It is a blot on our collective consciousness. One of the most visible and widespread is the trafficking of women and children for commercial sexual exploitation. The issue of the sexual exploitation of women and children is not new, as it goes back into the history, cultures and traditions of many societies. What is new is the unscrupulous and massive scale of the problem, exacerbated by globalisation, and modern technology and its link to a lucrative tourist sex industry. Trafficking is increasing dramatically in the Asian region, but the phenomenon spans the globe. While the fact of its existence is known to most of us, the enormity of the problem, its underpinning and its ramifications are often blurred.

With the progress of human civilization it was expected that man's interest in sex would diminish slowly. However, not only man's indulgence in sex has increased, but has crossed all the barriers of moral values and social norms. He has become more perverse, and has not spared even the innocent child in his pursuit of sexual pleasure. There could be few things that may be viewed as more obscene and abominable and that provoke as much public outrage as sexual crimes against children. Sadly, it is an organised crime now. These crimes though not overtly committed are suffered in silence and slowly corrode the social and moral fabric of a nation.

The institution of prostitution is as old as human civilization and the hyperbolic statement which refer to it as oldest profession conveys substantial truth. Today, it has assumed the proportion of multi-billion dollar industry, with children being bought and sold and traded like any other goods. Child prostitution is the worst of all forms of child abuse.

After illegal trafficking in drugs and weapons, human trafficking is the third biggest money earning international crime. It is estimated that over 27 million men, women and children all over the world are victims of human trafficking. India is concerned as one of the countries which are a source, a transit point, as well as a destination for trafficking in women and young children in South Asia. The problem in India is all the more severe not only because India is a poor country with around 35 per cent of India's population live below the poverty line, but also because India is surrounded by poor countries such as Nepal and Bangladesh wherein there is an easy availability of victims. The fact that India have open border with Nepal is a boon for traffickers and lack of strict vigil on Indo-Bangladesh border further aggravates the problem.

Before delving into the subject of 'child prostitution' it would be necessary to understand the meaning of two words 'child' and 'prostitution'. In common parlance child is a person, who because of his or her age, immature thought process and imperfect judgement is unable to comprehend the consequences of his/her own actions. Such a person is called a 'minor' under the Indian law. The Indian Penal Code says that a child may not be capable of forming any criminal intention up to a certain age and to that extent he/she enjoys immunity from any legal punishment. But beyond that age he/she may be liable for his/her acts and face punishment.

MEANING OF PROSTITUTION AND CHILD PROSTITUTION

In general sense prostitution is the setting one's self to sale or devoting to in famous purpose what is in one's power in its more restricted and legal sense, it is the practice of a female offering her body to an indiscriminate intercourse with man, as distinguished from sexual intercourse confined to one man, or as sometimes stated, common lewdness of a woman for game; the act of permitting a common and indiscriminate sexual intercourse.[1] The expression 'prostitute' means a woman who offers her body to indiscriminate sexual intercourse, especially for hire. Child prostitution refers to the sexual exploitation of a child for remuneration in cash or in kind, usually, but not always organised by an intermediary (parents, family members, procurers, etc.). The United Nations Convention on the Rights of Child, 1990, defines child prostitution as sexual exploitation of a child below the age of 18 years for remuneration in cash or kind.[2] The child prostitution is closely connected with child pornography. It refers to the visual or audio depiction of a child for the sexual gratification of the use, and involves the production, distribution and or use of such material.

Child prostitution has emerged in recent years as a global phenomenon of disquieting proportions. It is found in both developing and developed countries, although the numbers loom larger in the case of the former. Despite attempts to counter the situation, it remains daunting and intractable. In various parts of the world, the situation is deteriorating. The sexual exploitation of children has become more insidious because of its transfrontier nature. Children are increasingly sold and trafficked across frontiers between developing and developed countries, among developing and among developed countries. The spread of child prostitution world-wide is part and parcel of the less positive aspects of globalisation, and all continents of the globe deserve attention.

According to the 1989 United Nations Convention on the Rights of the Child the term "child" generally encompasses a person under 18 years of age.[3] A definition of child a prostitution can be explained from the 1990-94 reports of the United Nations Special Rapporteur on the Sale of children.[4]

The occurrence of child prostitution varies from individual cases to mass victims of organised crime. Some victims are runaways from home or State institutions, others are sold by their parents or forced or tricked into prostitution and others are street children. One tends to think first and foremost of young girls in the trade but there is an increase in the number of young boys engaged in prostitution. The most disquieting cases are those children who are forced into the trade and are then incarcerated. These children run the possible further risk of torture and subsequent death.

Causes of Child Prostitution

The problem of child prostitution in India is more complicated than in other Third World Countries where it is directly related to tourism. In India, sexual exploitation of children has its roots in traditional practices, beliefs and gender discrimination. The supply of girls for prostitution from one state to another state is very common and also supply of Indian girls to the countries to the West is not uncommon. It is estimated that nearly one lakh girls are brought from Nepal every year for the purpose of prostitution in India, over fifty per cent of them are minors. The factors those are responsible that lead the minors to the institution of prostitution are as follows:

Abduction: This is the most common cause. Young girls are abducted from their villages or native places on some or the other pretext exploiting their innocence. They are abducted or kidnapped from the places when they are going to movies, cities, temples, pilgrims, and often they are lured by making them film stars, offering job opportunities and marriages.

Child Pornography and Sex Tourism: Child pornography and sex tourism are closely interconnected, and are mutually reinforcing crimes. Sex tourists have been on the forefront in the production of pornographic material in the form of pictures, films, etc. depicting images of nude children and sex with children, mainly children from the developing countries—their safe destinations. They have also been instrumental in transferring pornographic material. Their work has become amazingly easier and safer with the advent of Internet technology. A child sexual exploiter invariably makes it a point to capture images of his prey, and likes to preserve and circulate the images. Pimps and pedophiles are using pornography to lure the young victims from non-traditional groups. In the traditional entertainer groups in many cities, nearly 60 per cent of the girl children have been introduced to the sex profession by their family members.[5]

The growth of the tourism industry has contributed to the increase in the sexual exploitation of the children, which often assumes intolerable forms. Tourism for purpose of sex has found its way into the mainstream tourism market.[6] Sex tourism involves travel agencies, tours operators, hotels and others in the tourism industry. Pedophiles are said to be the dominant 'Clientele' in sex tourism.[7]

Devadasi System: The inhuman system of prostitution with religious sanction, i.e. *devadasi* system still continues to flourish in the so called progressive and democratic country. Every year thousands of girls are dedicated to Goddess *Yellama* and *Renuka*, after a brief period of concubinage, they become accessible to urban prostitution. It is found that three socialised instruments perpetuate the fates of these women, namely economic organisation, brute force and religious rituals.

Superstitious Belief: High demand for virgin girls and young children motivate the traffickers to traffic in children. The pressure comes from clients as they feel it as safe sex and of the popular myth that sex with virgins can cure them of HIV and other serious diseases.[8] Rejection of condoms while exploiting children as sex objects was not merely a result of ignorance or lack of access to condoms. It was perhaps, a conscious decision to 'pass on' the sexually transmitted diseases to the child in order to get rid of the infection. Recent Indian Government statistics put the number of people infected with HIV at 3.5 million, indicating approximately three out of every 100 Indians are now infected with the virus which leads to AIDS. Almost 9 out of 10 of those people are below 45 years old.

Rape: About 6 per cent of the children coming to prostitution, come after the incidence of rape. Rape of the girls is a great social stigma and in some circumstances the victims of rape are not even accepted at home. Apart from the delay or even absence of justice, the victims have to face similar incidents every now and then. When they do not find any safe place in society and do not foresee any better future perspectives, they find their way into prostitution.

Incest: About 8 per cent of children came to prostitution because of the incidence of Incest.[9] The most common incest is between father and daughter, followed by uncle-niece and even sometimes brother's friends. When the young victim of incest is exploited at home, she does not foresee safety anywhere else in the society and slowly ends up into prostitution. There are circumstances where it has been found that girls were sold by their father or uncle or the brother-in-law.

Marriage: Girls also enter into prostitution due to marriage or fake marriages. In our patriarchal society, man having an upper hand often desert the woman after staying with her for a short time or may pass her into the hands of traffickers or exploiters.

CHILD PROSTITUTION — THE ULTIMATE DENIAL OF HUMAN RIGHTS

Human Rights are the basic and absolute rights that every person has because he or she is a human being. They recognise the vulnerability of the human being in civil, political, economic, social and cultural processes and provide protection. Every human being has this right although the extent to which they can be enforced in practice varies from country to country. These rights come along with having duties and responsibilities. In preserving the freedom, rights and justice for all, everyone has responsibility to abide by the law and everyone has duties in the community. In exercising freedoms and rights, everyone must also respect the rights and freedoms of others.

Trading in human beings and their exploitation in varied forms by traffickers in human being is one of the most despicable forms of violation of human rights. Trafficking in its widest sense includes not just exploitation of others or services, slavery or practices similar to slavery or trade in human beings. Child prostitution clearly violates the fundamental right to a life with dignity. It also violates right to health care, right to liberty and security of person, right to freedom from torture, violence, cruelty or degrading treatment. While societies may vary in their ideas on childhood and child development, one thing that all can agree on is the importance of the well-being of children. It is well recognised everywhere that children need special care and protection for healthy development because of their special needs and vulnerability. Special instruments have been drawn up to safeguard and enforce child rights. The recognised standard is the Convention on the Rights of the Child,[10] which was drawn up in 1989 and has been ratified by almost all countries in the world.

Dr. K.K. Mukhopadhyay, Prof. from Delhi School of Social Work, Delhi University, in his presentation held on November 19, 1995 on National Consultation on Child Prostitution, said that young girls in India were taken away from their parents in poor backward and drought affected districts of the country for the purposes of trafficking. According to him, about eighty per cent of the girls who were in this profession entered it as children, due to difficult circumstances, such as poverty, illiteracy, ignorance and deception. The increasingly consumerist society only further complicated the situation. Children are often hired or are sold by their families to agents who may or may not reveal the true nature of the work offered. Sometimes, the young girls are deceived by young urban boy who go to the villages where they conduct fake marriages with these girls. They bring them to the cities and sell them to the brothels.

The Convention on the Rights of the Child clearly lays down the role of the States in the prostitution of the child in Article 34,[11] where it notes that the states will undertake to protect the child from all forms of sexual exploitation and abuse. Articles 35[12] and 36[13] states that all appropriate national, bilateral and multilateral measures will be taken by the State to prevent abduction, sale and trafficking in children, coercion to engage in unlawful sexual activity and all forms of exploitation such as prostitution or pornographic performances. It also states that all children must receive the opportunity to discover their identity and realise their self-worth in a safe and supportive environment.

When a child is sexually exploited, one question comes to the mind that what is his or her childhood? The very basis of the child sex industry designating of a child as a commodity for sale and purchase demeans and dehumanises the child. It also serves the sexual drive of sexually immature men who seek emotional release by exploiting a completely powerless slave child.

The sexual exploitation of children does not occur in a vacuum, but involves a more widespread exploitation, sexual or otherwise. Poverty and ignorance are the underlying causes of this world-wide phenomenon, as families rely on their youngest members to contribute to the household income. The child in prostitution is a victim of pedophiles who pose as tourists, and of traffickers who forces them into this trade.

Child prostitution is a term in popular usage, but is inaccurate because it implies consent. And a child does not consent. He or she is rather victimised into sexual slavery. All over the world, the child's vulnerability to commercial sexual exploitation lies in his or her family circumstances. The majority of sexually exploited children are either from marginalised families in the cities and destitute families in the country or children of women already in sex industry.

In India, systems of child prostitution as varied as the *Devadasi* or the *Jogini*, and the trafficking system that makes young girls across South Asia and into urban centres, reveal the active exploitation and the socio-economic realities that make such exploitation possible. Within last few years, some instances of sexual abuse of children have also come to light in popular tourist destinations. About 85 per cent of the prostitutes in Delhi and Calcutta were compelled into trade when very young. Entertaining about seven to eight clients in one day, often during heavy menstrual periods, ice is used and they are forced to receive clients. Physical or psychological torture may be specifically employed to ensure compliance in many cases.[14]

Dr. John Rhode, UNICEF representative in India, in his opening speech observed that *with the exception of outright death, child prostitution is the ultimate denial of the child transforming his entire life*. Any society that tolerates this cannot afford to call itself civilized. In India, there are some myths that men seek young girls, believing that sex with virgins can cure sexually transmitted diseases, employing that younger sex workers are less likely to carry HIV. On the contrary, a child's immature body and inadequately developed immune systems make her more susceptible to sexually transmitted and other diseases.

An irony of the tourist sex industry in all its manifestations is that the poverty which drives a child to offer sex for money, offers the sex tourist an easy opportunity to expiate guilt. By paying for a child's services he can convince himself that he is helping her and her family to escape economic hardship. It has been found that twenty five thousand children in Brazil, thirty thousand children in Sri Lanka, forty thousand children in Philippines, three hundred thousand children in Thailand, four hundred thousand children in India, all engaged in child prostitution and hundred thousand children in the United States of America.[15]

People think of themselves civilized living in modern times, yet child prostitution is growing problem in both developing and developed countries. It represents the ultimate betrayal of our commitment to human decency and respect. Child prostitution is an attack on humanity that focuses exclusively on the next generation. It subjects children to emotional and physical dangers that can leave scars for a life time. There are many factors, which leads to child into prostitution. They are poverty, the disintegration of families, incest and domestic violence. But one factor is clear that somebody, somewhere made a conscious decision to force a child into prostitution, and this decision was made by a growing demand for child prostitutes, both domestically and from international sex rings and sex tourism. Ultimately the goal of these rings is one thing — money. In the poorest societies, children are often sold by their families in a desperate attempt to get money. Some are kidnapped or lured by traffickers with promises of employment in the city, only to end up in brothels. In fact, in many countries young girls are often viewed as less valuable, even in their own families. The resulting discrimination sometimes leads to their sale into prostitution by those same families. Little boys are not immune either. They are forced into prostitution to satisfy a growing demand for young males.

Child prostitution hurts children both physically and emotionally. Many child prostitutes contract AIDS and other diseases. Many are beaten. There are some reports that children are tattooed by organised crime elements that control them as property. The emotional toll on these kids is immeasurable. Child prostitution undermines a child's development and robs a child of his or her dignity and basic human rights. A child in that situation can never look at an advent, at a fellow human being, in the same way. These scars will last for ever. Moreover, advances in technology like the Internet have increased the opportunities available for those who seek sex from children.[16]

Indian Laws

The Constitution of India requires positive steps to be taken by policy makers for the protection of the weaker sections of the society. The fundamental rights enshrined in the Constitution also take care of special position of women and children. Article 23 provides right against exploitation.[17] This article embodies two declarations. First, the traffic in human beings, beggar and other similar forms of forced labour are prohibited. The prohibition applies not only to State but also to private persons, bodies and organisations. Second, any contravention of the prohibition shall be an offence punishable in accordance with law. Under Article 35 of the Constitution laws punishing acts prohibited by this article shall only be made by Parliament, though existing laws on the subject, until altered or repealed by Parliament, are saved. The judiciary in *Raj Bahadur* vs. *Legal Remembrancer*[18] held that traffic in women for immoral purposes is prohibited under Article 23.

The Directive Principles of State Policy serve as the guiding star for various social welfare legislations passed in favour of women. They assert that all the citizens have the right to adequate means of livelihood. According to Article 39(e) the health and strength of workers, men, women and the tender age of children should not be abused.[19] It tries to ensure that citizens are not forced by economic necessity to enter into vocations unsuited to their age or strength. Article 38 which is more social welfare oriented states that the State is to secure a social order in which justice social, economic and political shall inform all the institutions of the national life.[20] It is a directive to the State to give effect to the objectives expressed in the Preamble to the Constitution, by securing a social order for the promotion of the welfare of the people. It is the star by which we are expected to chart our course. It is to achieve the goals echoed in Article 38 that Part IV contains various provisions. The concept of social justice, which the Constitution engrafted, consists of diverse principles essential for the orderly growth and development of personality of every citizen. Thus, social justice is a dynamic device to mitigate the sufferings of the children who are trafficked for commercial sexual exploitation in the society.

The *Suppression of Immoral Traffic in Women and Girls Act 1956*, proved to be inadequate to combat the increasing commercialisation of trafficking. Parliament amended the law in 1970 and later in 1986. The Suppression of Immoral Traffic in Women and Girls Act 1956 was amended by The Suppression of Immortal Traffic in Women and Girls (Amendment) Act 1978 (46 of 1978) w.e.f. 2 October, 1979; and The Suppression of Immortal Traffic in Women and Girls (Amendment) Act 1986 (44 of 1986) w.e.f. 26 January, 1987.

Under Section 8 of PITA the prostitute is treated as a criminal. Fortunately this Act recognises that children and even men can be sexually abused for commercial purposes and should be protected.

Section 2 of this Act makes the definition of brothel[21] wider to include any place used for the purpose of sexual exploitation or abuse. This broader definition of brothel will make it easier to prosecute the brothel keeper under Section 3 of the Act. Now landlords, tenants and other occupants of the premises may not escape punishment for brothel keeping under the defence of ignorance. The punishment for living on the earnings of child prostitute has been increased. There is an increase in the prison term for offenders convicted of procuring minors. Life imprisonment is the maximum punishment ordained when it is committed against minors or children. Section 9 of this Act[22] provides greater punishment to persons who cause, aid or abet the seduction of women and girls, over whom they have authority or who are in their care and custody, for prostitution.

This Act empowers the Central Government to appoint trafficking officers. These special police officers can search without warrant any premises where this offence is suspected of being committed, and they can rescue any person who is being forced into prostitution or is carrying on or is being made to carry on prostitution. Discretionary powers have been given to the magistrates for interim placement of children and minors who are rescued, in an institution recognised under the Children's Act. Provisions for protective and corrective homes for the safe custody of children and special courts for their speedy trial are some of the encouraging changes that are sought to be achieved by the new Act.

By the use of presumptions, the burden of the prosecution is lightened by the IPTA 1986. There are certain presumptions under the Act in form of the child victims. These are:

- If a child is found in a brothel or under suspicious circumstances[23] in the custody of a person, other than the parent or lawful guardian who is unable to explain satisfactorily the presence of such a child, that person shall be presumed to have procured the child for the purposes of prostitution.
- A report in a newspaper on the use of certain premises as a brothel is deemed to be sufficient proof of the landlord, occupier or tenant knowingly allowing such use.
- If a child is found accompanying in suspicious circumstance, a person who is neither its parent or lawful guardian and who is leaving the country, that person is committing the offence of immoral trafficking.

Rescue and Rehabilitation of Children and Minors under the ITPA 1986

When a magistrate has reason to believe from information received from the police or from any other person authorised by the state government that any person is living on, or is caring on, or is being made to carry on prostitution in a brothel, he may direct a police officer not below the mark of sub-inspector to enter such brothel and to remove such person and produce the person before him.[24] A minor as a child rescued under the Juvenile Justice Act 1986, is treated as a neglected child.[25] Which is also known as Child in need of care and protection, now the Juvenile Justice (Care and Protection of Children) Act 2000, and has to be produced before the Juvenile Welfare Board,[26] now the Child Welfare Committee for reception and rehabilitation, and placing in safe custody. The Committee shall consist of a Chairperson and four other members as the State Government may think fit to appoint, of whom at least one shall be a woman and another an expert on matters concerning children. The qualifications of the Chairperson and the members and the tenure for which they may be appointed shall be such as may be prescribed. The appointment of any member of the committee may be terminated after holding inquiry, by the State Government, if he has been found guilty of misuse of power vested under this Act; he has been convicted of an offence involving moral turpitude and such conviction has not been reversed or he has not been granted full pardon in respect of such offence; he fails to attend the proceedings of the committee for consecutive three months without any valid reason or he fails to attend less than three-forth of the sittings in a year. The Committee shall function as a Bench of Magistrates and shall have the powers conferred by the Code of Criminal Procedure, 1973 (2 of 1974) on a Metropolitan Magistrate or, as the case may be, a Judicial Magistrate of the first class — Section 29 of Juvenile Justice Act. There is a provision for providing for intermediate custody in a shelter home or corrective institution after rescue pending detailed inquiry.

The ***Criminal Procedure Code of 1973*** also protects girls from sexual exploitation. It states that a presiding Judge or District Magistrate may, upon complaint that a female child under the age of eighteen years is abducted or unlawfully detained, order the immediate restoration[27] of the girl to her liberty or to her parent, guardian or husband. Section 98 is intended to give immediate relief to a woman or girl abducted or detained for any lawful purpose. An action under this section cannot be taken except upon complaint made an oath.

Section 366 A of the ***Indian Penal Code 1860*** makes procreation of a minor girl from one part of place to another is punishable[28] and Section 366B, which makes importation of a girl below the age of twenty one years punishable.[29] These sections try to prevent prostitutions by strict penal action. Sections 372[30] and 373 make selling and buying of girls of any age for the purpose of prostitution, a heinous crime, for which even ten years imprisonment and fine can be awarded. These sections conjointly punish both the giver as well as the receiver of minor girls for immoral purpose, illicit sexual intercourse or prostitution. Section 372 protects the minors even against her own parents or other lawful guardians. Section 373[31] strikes at the keepers of brothels and all others who rely on the profits arising from the general prostitution of girls. The Section is primarily intended to prohibit the purchase of minors from third parties, and it is unquestionable that the buying or hiring does not ordinarily import purchase or hire of an object as distinct from the vendor. The two sections are, however, intended to save young person's below the age of eighteen from being trafficked for the purpose of prostitution. Section 374[32] provides punishment for compelling any person to labour against the will of that person. So no child can be allowed to work forcefully even if the employment of the person is for immoral purpose.

Summary

The human rights of child are an inalienable, integral and indivisible part of universal human rights. Trafficking in children is one of the worst, the most brazen abuses of human rights. It is a matter of shame that even after half a century since the adoption of the Declaration of Human Rights by the global community, trafficking continues to thrive. One of the most visible and widespread is the trafficking of women and children for commercial sexual exploitation. The issue of the sexual exploitation of children is not new, as it goes back into the history, cultures and traditions of many societies. What is new is the unscrupulous and massive scale of the problem, exacerbated by globalisation and its links to a lucrative tourist and sex industry. Thus, as a result, it is little known fact that a modern development tool like tourism also contributes to the exploitation of children in many ways — child sexual exploitation and commodification of children that leads to commercial sexual exploitation of children, are prominent among these. Trafficking is increasing dramatically in the Asia region, but the phenomenon spans the globe. While the fact of its existence is known to most of us, the enormity of the problem, its underpinnings and its ramifications are often blurred. Child prostitution. It may be said that the numbers of child victims in prostitution are highest in Asia.

NOTES

1. The Encyclopedia Law Dictionary Legal Maxims, *Latin Terms, Words and Phrases*, 2nd Edition, 1997.
2. U.N. Convention on the Rights of the Child, New York, 1990.
3. Article 1 of CRC reads — For the purpose of the present convention, a child means every human being below the age of eighteen years, unless, under the law applicable to the child majority is attained earlier.
4. Child Prostitution means the sexual exploitation of a child for remuneration in cash or in kind usually but not always organised by an intermediary (parent, family member, teacher, etc.).
5. *The Times of India*, November 10, 1998.
6. Department of Women and Child Development (DWCD) 1997-98, *Annual Report*, DWCD, Ministry Development, Government of India.
7. Desai, Nishtha, 2001. *Tourism Related Pedophile in Goa*, Vikas Adhyayan Kendra, Mumbai, pp. 38-41.
8. Mostly in the State of Andhra Pradesh, Karnataka and Maharashtra girls are dedicated to *Yellamma* moon day of *Chaitra* (March-April) or *Magh* (November-December) months at temples.
9. Incest: Sexual Intercourse between persons so closely related that they are by customary law forbidden to marry.
10. The General Assembly of United Nations adopted the Convention on the Rights of the Child on 20th November, 1989. It bears the opinion regarding protection of children everywhere against exploitation, neglect and abuse. Within five years the Convention has been ratified by 186 nations. The Convention draws attention to four sets of civil, political, social, economic and cultural rights of every child. These includes: The Right to Survival, the Right to Protection, the Right to Development and the Right to Participation.
11. Article 34 of CRC reads — State parties undertakes to protect the child from all forms of sexual exploitation and sexual abuse. For these purposes State parties shall in particular take all appropriate national, bilateral and multi-lateral measures to prevent:
    (a) The inducement or coercion of a child to engage in any unlawful sexual activity.
    (b) The exploitative use of children in prostitution or other unlawful sexual activity.
    (c) The exploitative use of children in pornographic performances and materials.
12. Article 35 of CRC reads — State parties shall take all appropriate national, bilateral and multilateral measures to prevent the abduction of, the sale of or traffic in children for any purpose or in any form.
13. Article 36 of CRC reads — State parties shall protect the child against all other forms of exploitation prejudicial to any aspects of the child's welfare.

14. Khan, Ali Mumtaz, 1996. *Street Girl and Immoral Traffic in India* — under the auspices of Centre for Research and Development of Dalits, Bangalore, Uppal Publishing House, New Delhi.
15. Paper from a symposium co-sponsored by the U.S. Department of Labour, Bureau of International Labour Affairs, the Women's Bureau, and the U.S. Department of State, Bureau of Democracy, Human Rights and Labour, held on September 29, 1995 at the U.S. Department of Labour in Washington, D.C.
16. The Sound of Silence — An introduction to basic psychotherapeutic skill for forming a relation with Adolescent and Survivors of Commercial Sexual Exploitation and Support by Saarthak and UNIFEM, New Delhi 2002, pp. 2-3.
17. *Article 23:* Prohibition of Traffic in Human Beings and Forced Labour —

    (i) Traffic in human beings and beggar and other similar forms of forced labour are prohibited and any contravention of this provision shall be an offence punishable in accordance with law.

    (ii) Nothing in this article shall prevent the State from imposing compulsory service for public purposes, and in imposing such service the state shall not make any discrimination on grounds only of religion, race, caste or class or any of them.

18. AIR 1953 Cal 522.
19. **Article 39(e) of Indian Constitution:** The State shall, in particular, direct its policy towards securing that the health and strength of workers, men and women and the tender age of children are not abused and that citizens are not forced by economic necessity to enter avocations unsuited to their age or strength.
20. **Article 38:** State to secure a social order for the promotion of welfare of the people — (i) The State shall strive the welfare of the people by securing and protecting as effectively as it may a social order in which justice, social, economic and political, shall inform all the institutions of the national life. (ii) The State shall, in particular, strive to minimise the inequalities in income, and endear our to eliminate inequalities in status, facilities and opportunities, not only amongst individuals, but also amongst groups of people residing in different areas or engaged in different vocations.
21. 'Brothel' includes any house, room, conveyance, on place or any portion of any house, room, conveyance, or place which is used for purpose of sexual exploitation or abuse for the gain of another person or for the mutual gain of two or more prostitutes — Section 2(a) ITPA 1986.
22. **Seduction of a Person in Custody** — Any person who having the custody, change or care of, or a position of authority over any person, cause or aids or abets the seduction for prostitution of that person shall be punishable on conviction with imprisonment of either description for a term which shall not be less than seven years but which may be for life or for a term which may extend to ten years and shall also be liable to fine: Provided that the court may for adequate and special reasons to the mentioned in the judgment impose a sentence of imprisonment for a term of less than seven years. — Section 9 of ITPA.
23. Suspicious circumstances in this section includes situations in which (i) the mother tongue of the accused is different from that of the child or the language is different from that generally spoken in the locality, (ii) where the child is wrongfully spoken in the locality, (ii) where the child is wrongfully confined without access to others, and (iii) where the child is married to a foreigner.

24. Rescue of Person — (1) Where a Magistrate has reason to believe from information received from the police or from any other person authorised by the State Government in this behalf or otherwise that any person is living, or is carrying on, not below the rank of a sub-inspector to enter such brothel, and to remove therefrom such person and produce him before him; (2) The police officer, after removing the person shall forthwith produce him before the Magistrate issuing the order.
25. "Child in need of care and protection" means a child —
    Who is found without any home or settled place or abode and without any ostensible means of subsistence, Who resides with a person (whether a guardian of the child or not) and such person — (a) has threatened to kill or injure the child and there is a reasonable likelihood of the threat being carried out, or (b) has killed abused or neglected some other child or children and there is a reasonable likelihood of the child in question killed abused or neglected by that person,
    Who is mentally or physically challenged or ill children or children suffering from terminal diseases or incurable diseases having no one to support or look after,
    Who has a parent or guardian and such parent or guardian is unfit or incapacitated to exercise control over the child,
    Who does have parent and no one is willing to take care of or whose parents have abandoned him or who is missing and run away child and whose parents cannot be found after reasonable injury,
    Who is being or likely to be grossly abused, tortured or exploited for the purpose of sexual abuse or illegal acts,
    Who is found vulnerable and is likely to be inducted into drug abuse of trafficking,
    Who is being or is likely to be abused for unconscionable gains.
26. Child welfare committee — The State Government may by notification in Official Gazette, constitute for every district or group of district, specified in the notification, one or more child Welfare Committees for exercising the powers and discharge the duties conferred on such committees in relation to child in need of care and protection under Juvenile Justice Act.
27. **Power to Compel Restoration of Abducted Females** — Upon complaint made on both of the abduction or unlawful detention of a woman or a female child under the age of eighteen years for any lawful purpose a District Magistrate, Sub-Divisional Magistrate or Magistrate of the first class any make an order for the immediate restoration of such woman to he liberty or of such female child to her husband/parent/guardian or other person having the lawful charge of such child and may compel compliance with such order using such force as may be necessary. — Section 98 of Cr.P.C.
28. **Procuration of Minor Girl** — Whoever, by any means whatsoever, induces any minor girl under the age of eighteen years to go from any place or to do any act with intent that such girl may be, or knowing that it is likely that she will be, forced or seduced to illicit intercourse with another person, shall be punishable with imprisonment which may extend to ten years, and shall also be liable to fine. — Section 366 A of IPC 1860.
29. **Importation of Girl from Foreign Country** — Whoever imports into (India) from any country outside India [or from the State of Jammu and Kashmir] and girl under the age of twenty-one years with intent that she may be or knowing it to be likely that she will be, forced or seduced to illicit intercourse with another

person, shall be punishable with imprisonment which may extend to ten years and shall also be liable to fine. — Section 366B of IPC 1860.

30. **Selling Minor for Purposes of Prostitution, etc.** — Whoever sells, lets to hire, or otherwise disposes of any 'person under the age of eighteen years with intent that such person shall at any age be employed or used for the purpose of prostitution or illicit intercourse with any person or for any unlawful and immoral purpose, of knowing it to be likely that such person will at any age be employed or used for any such purpose, shall be punished with imprisonment of either description for a term which may extend to ten years, and shall be liable to fine.

   Explanation 1. When a female under the age of eighteen years is sold, let for hire, or otherwise disposed of to a prostitute or to any person who keeps or manages a brothel, the person so disposing of such female shall, until the contrary is proved, be presumed to have disposed of her with the intent that she shall be used for the purpose of prostitution.

   Explanation 2. For the purposes of this section "illicit intercourse" means sexual intercourse between persons not united by marriage or by any union or by any union or tie which, though not amounting to a marriage, is recognised by the personal law or custom of the community to which they belong or, where they belong to different communities, of both such communities, as constituting between them a quasi — marital relation. — Section 372 of IPC.

31. **Buying Minor for Purpose of Prostitution, etc.** Whoever buys, hires or otherwise obtains possession of any person under the age of eighteen years with intent that such person shall at any age be employed or used for the purpose of prostitution or illicit intercourse with any person or for any unlawful and immoral purpose, of knowing it to be likely that such person will at any age be employed or used for any purpose, shall be punished within imprisonment of either description for a term which may extend to ten years, and shall also be liable to fine.

   Explanation 1. Any prostitute or any person keeping or managing a brothel, who buys, hires or otherwise obtains possession of a female under the age of eighteen years shall, until the contrary is proved, be presumed to have obtained possessions of such female with the intent that she shall be used for the purpose of prostitution.

   Explanation 2. "Illicit intercourse" has the same meaning as in Section 372. — Section 373 IPC.

32. **Unlawful Compulsory Labour** — Whoever unlawfully compels any person to labour against the will of that person, shall be punished with imprisonment of either description for a term which may extend to one year, or with fine, or with both. — Section 374 of IPC.

BIBLIOGRAPHY

Books

Advani Poornima, Lina Gonslaves and J.K. Mittal, 2006. *Rape — A Legal Study*, New Delhi: National Commission for Women.

Austin, Granville, 1960. *Indian Constitution: Cornerstone of a Nation*, Bombay: Oxford University Press.

Bajpai, Asha, 2003. *Child Rights in India*, New Delhi: Oxford University.

Baligar, Vinaya; Prabha, V., 1999. *Mother and Girl Child*, Jaipur: Rawat Publications.

Basu, Malika, 2006. "Gender Focus in Resettlement Planning", in Hari Mohan Mathur (ed.), *Managing Resettlement in India*, New Delhi: Oxford University Press.

Baxi, Upendra, 1986. *Toward a Sociology of Law*, Delhi: Satavahana.

Bhadra, Mita, 1999. *Girl Child in Indian Society*, Jaipur: Rawat Publications.

Bhatia, S.C., 1988. *Social Audit of Immoral Traffic Prevention Act*, Delhi: University of Delhi.

Chakraborthy, Kakolee, 2000. *Women as Devadasis — Origin and Growth of the Devadasi Profession*, New Delhi: Deep & Deep Publications Pvt. Ltd.

Chandra, Sudhir, 1998. *Enslaved Daughter*, New Delhi: Oxford University Press.

Deb, Sibnath and Mukherjee Aparna, 2009. *Impact of Sexual Abuse on Mental Health of Children*, New Delhi: Concept Publishing Co.

Debabrata, R., 1997. *Lost Childhood — The First Survey of Prostitution in Delhi*, New Delhi: National Commission for Women.

Dreze, Jean and Sen, Amartya, 2004. "Gender Inequality and Women's Agency in Caste, Class, Gender", in Manoranjan Mohanty (ed.), New Delhi: Sage Publications.

Dube, Dipa, 2008. *Rape Laws in India*, New Delhi: Butterworths.

Gathia, Joseph, 1999. *Child Prostitution in India*, New Delhi: Concept Publishing Company.

Ghosh, Biswajit, (ed.), 2011. *Interrogating Development — Discourses on Development in India Today*, Jaipur: Rawat Publication.

Goswami, Sambodh, 2007. *Female Infanticide and Child Marriage*, Jaipur: Rawat Publication.

Itzin, C., 1992. *Pornography: Women, Violence and Civil Liberty*, Oxford University Press.

Iyer, V.K. Krishna, 1979. *Of Law and Life*, New Delhi: Vikas Publishing House.

Jain, Atul, 2005. *Cyber Crime*, New Delhi: Isha Books.

Jain, Devaki, 1980. *Women Quest for Power: Five Indian Case Studies*, Ghaziabad: Vikas Publishing House.

Jain, M.P., 2015. *Indian Constitutional Law*, Haryana: Lexis Nexis.

Jairam, K., 2004. *Sociology and Social Change*, Delhi: Dominant Publications Distributors.

Joardar, B., 1984. *Prostitution — A Bibliographical Synthesis*, New Delhi: Inter-India Publications.

Joseph, B. Ramola, 2007. "Widowhood and Law in India", in Kamal K. Misra and Janet Huber Lowry (ed.), *Recent Studies on Indian Women*, Jaipur: Rawat Publications.

Joshi, Madhu (ed.), 1997. *Women and Children in Prostitution — Human Right Perspectives*, New Delhi: Joint Women Programme.

Julia, R. and Herman Schewendinger, 1993. *Rape and Inequality*, California: Sage Publications.

Karlekar, M., 2003. "Domestic Violence", in Veena Das (ed.), *The Oxford Indian Companion to Sociology and Social Anthropology*, New Delhi: Oxford University Press.

Krishna, S., 1996. *Restoring Childhood — The Commonwealth Human Right Initiative*, New Delhi: Konark Publishers Pvt. Ltd.

Krishnakumari, N.S., 1987. *Status of Single Women in India*, New Delhi: Uppal Publishing House.

Kumar, Pankaj and Sadhna Gupta, 2015. *Relocating Women's Equality*, Jaipur: Rawat Publication.

Mathur, Hari Mohan, 2009. "Gender Biases in Resettlement Planning", in Lyla Mehta (ed.), *Displaced by Development*, New Delhi: Sage Publication.

Mehta, L., 2000. "Women Facing Submergence: Displacement and Resistance in the Narmada Valley", in V. Damodaran and M. Unnithan Kumar (ed.), *Post Colonial India: History, Political and Culture*, New Delhi: Manohar.

Menon Madhava, (ed.), 1991. *Rights of the Child*, Bangalore: NLSIU.

Mishra, Lakshmidhar, 2000. *Child Labour in India*, New Delhi: Oxford University.

Mitra, Aloka, 2000. *Prevention of Trafficking in Children in the Red Light Areas*, Kolkata: Women's Waterlink Foundation.

Panigrahi, Lalita, 1972. *British Social Policy and Female Infanticide in India*, New Delhi: Munshiram Manoharlal.

Rao, Mamta, 2005. *Women and Children*, New Delhi: Eastern Book Company.

Paranjape, N.V., 2005. *Criminology and Penology*, Allahabad: Central Law Publications.

Paul, M., 1986. *Dowry and Position of Women in India: A Study of Delhi Metropolis*, New Delhi: Inter-India Publications.

Sarkar, Sumita and Manjari Srivastava, 2011. *Globalization and Gender*, Jaipur: Rawat Publications.

Saxena, Poonam Pradhan, 2007. *Family Law*, New Delhi: Lexis Nexis.

Shamim, Ishrat, 1998. *Trafficking and Sexual Exploitation of Children — A Bangladesh Perspective*, Bangladesh: Centre for Women and Children Studies.

Sharma, A., 2004. *Hinduism and Human Rights: A conceptual Approach*, New Delhi: Oxford University Press.

Sharma, A.K., 2007. *Child Labour*, New Delhi: Anmol Publications Pvt. Ltd.

Sherwani, A., 1998. *The Girl Child Crisis*, New Delhi: India Social Institute.

Shrivastava, M.P., 2006. *Child Labour Laws in India*, Allahabad: Law Publishing House.

Sinha, Rajeev Kumar, 2009. *Child Labour in Unorganised Sector*, New Delhi: Shree Publications & Distributions.

Sinha, Swapan Kumar, 1991. *Child Labour in Calcutta: A Sociological Study*, Kolkata: Naya Prokash.

Tandon, R.K. and K.N. Sudrashan, 1997. *Child Prostitution*, Delhi: A.P.H. Publishing Corporation.

Thapan, M., 1997. *Embodiment Essays on Gender and Identity in Feminity and Its Discontents: Womens Body in Intimate Relationship*, New Delhi: Oxford University Press.

The World Bank, 2004. *Reaching Out to the Child — An Integrated Approach to Child Development*, New Delhi: Oxford University Press.

Tripathy, P.C., 2000. *Crime Against Women*, New Delhi: APH Publishing Corp.

Venkataramiah, E.S. (ed.), 1998. *Human Rights in the Changing World*, Bangalore: B.V. Naga Publishers.

Venkateswaran, Sandhya, 1995. *Environment, Development and the Gender Gap*, New Delhi: Sage Publications.

Yatindra, Singh, 2007. *Cyber Laws*, New Delhi: Universal Law Publishing Co.

Journal

Aguayo, Victor; Singh, Gayatri and Badgaiyan, Nina, 2014. "Scoring Child Nutrition in India", *Economic and Political Weekly*, April 5, Vol. XLIX.

Awais, Mohammad, Tosib Alam and Mohd. Asif, 2009. "Socio-Economic Empowerment of Tribal Women: An Indian Perspective", *International Journal of Rural Studies*, Vol. 16, No. 1: 1-11.

B. Vijachandran Pillai and V. Hari Kumar, 2006. "Self-Help Groups in Kerala", Kurukshetra, Vol. 54, July, No. 9.

Basu, S.K., 1993. "Health Status of Tribal Women in India", *Social Change*, 23(4): 19-39.

Bhasin, Veena, 2007. "Status of Tribal Women in India", *Studies of Home and Community Science*, 1(1): 1-16.

Das, Achyut and Vindhya Das, 1992. "Development and Tribal Women", *Economic and Political Weekly*, 27(27): 1372-73.

D'Cunha, Jean, 1987. "Prostitution in a Patriarchal Society — A Critical Review of the SITA Act", *Economic and Political Weekly*, 7 November.

Desai, A.R., 1985. "Women's Movement in India: As Assessment", *Economic and Political Weekly*, Vol. 20, pp. 992-95, June 8.

Desai, Mihir, 2011. "Land Acquisition Law and the Proposed Changes", *Economic and Political Weekly*, 46 (26 ^ 27): 95-100.

Deshpande, Sudha and L.K. Deshpande, 1992. "New Economic Policy and Female Employment", *Economic and Political Weekly*, October 10, 1992.

Ganguli, Geetanjali, 1998. "The Regulation of Women's Sexuality through Law — Civil and Criminal Laws", *Economic and Political Weekly*, 7 March.

Ganguly Thukral, Enakshi, 1996. "Development, Displacement and Rehabilitation: Locating Gender", *Economic and Political Weekly*, 31(24): 1500-03.

Giri, Mohini, 2001. "Trafficking in Women and Children", *The Journal of Women's Empowerment*, 16(1), January-March.

Jena, K.C., 2012. "Female Feoticide and Infanticide in India: The Emerging Issues", *Indian Bar Council Review*, Vol. XXXIX (1).

Joshi, Madhu, 2002. "The Matrix — Commercial Sexual Exploitation in India", *The Little Magazine*, Vol. III, Issue 4: 35-37.

Menon, Geeta, 1987, "Tribal Women: Victims of the Development Process", *Social Action*, Vol. 37(4): 373-90.

Menon, Nivedita, 2004. "Refusing Globalization and the Authentic Nation: Feminist Politics in Current Conjuncture", *Economic and Political Weekly*, January 3.

Ministry of Statistics and Programme Implementation, 2012. *Children in India 2012—A Statistical Appraisal*, Social Statistics Division, Central Statistics Office, Government of India.

Nagpal, Jitendra, 2016. "The Psychological Challenges in Educating Adolescents", *Yojana*, January, Vol. 60.

Pal, C., 1981. "Basic Framework for Child Welfare under Indian Constitution", *7 Kurukshetra Law Journal*, 90.

Patel, Amrit, 2016. "Potential of Beti Bachao, Beti Padhao Programme", *Kurukshetra*, January, Vol. 64, No. 3.

Patil, Shivraj, 2000. "Children — Supreme Asset of the Nation", *AIR Journal*, 49.

Ramchandran, Vimala, 2016. "Women and Girls' Education", *Yojana*, January, Vol. 60.

Roy Burman, J.J., 2012. "Status of Tribal Women in India", *Mainstream Weekly*, Vol. L, No. 12.

Sharma, Sarla, 2001. "Issues in International Sexual Trafficking in Women", *Asian Women*, Vol. 13: 37-59.

Shefalee, Vasudev, 2003. "Cover Story — Girls for Sale", *India Today*, 3 October.

Shiva, Vandana and Jayanta Bandyopadhyay, 1986. "The Evolution, Structure, and Impact of the Chipko Movement", *Mountain Research and Development*, 6(2), 133-42.

Singh, Rattan and Gagandeep Kaur, 2009. "Human Rights of Indigenous People: A Reflection of Reality", *Asia-Pacific Journal of Social Sciences*, I(1): 117-26.

Srivastsa, P., 2016. "Girl Child Issues: Need to Ensure Stringent Policies", *Kurukshetra*, January, Vol. 64, No. 3.

INDEX